THE
CELTIC FC
MISCELLANY

THE
CELTIC FC
MISCELLANY

DAVID POTTER

The
History
Press

First published in 2012 by

The History Press
The Mill, Brimscombe Port
Stroud, Gloucestershire, GL5 2QG
www.thehistorypress.co.uk

British Library Cataloguing in Publication Data.
A catalogue record for this book is available from the British Library.

ISBN 978 0 7524 6462 6

Typesetting and origination by The History Press
Printed in Great Britain

INTRODUCTION

It has been a singular and peculiar pleasure for me to write this miscellany of Celtic Football Club. Far too often, writers tend to become over-concerned about players' appearances for the club, goalscoring records and the 'heavy' stuff of football. There is of course a place for this, but one must not also lose sight of the light-hearted, offbeat and humorous side of football.

Celtic Football Club is such a vast organisation and it is now over fifty years since Glen Daly recorded 'The Celtic Song' with the lyrics, 'if you know their history, it's enough to make your heart go oh-oh-oh-oh . . .' Some think that the word 'sad' should be there instead of 'oh-oh-oh-oh', but if this is the case, the word 'sad' can only really apply in the emotional, tears-springing-to-your-eyes sense of the word, for there is nothing about Celtic that really should make anyone sad. It is a magnificent example of how, in the early days at least, an ethnic minority, underprivileged and discriminated against, simply decided to do something about it. There was no real mileage to be got from moaning and self-pity; far better to build the best football team in the world!

Times have of course changed, and Celtic's support is now drawn from all social classes, nationalities and ethnic groups, proving (long before Western society acknowledged it) that what Walfrid and Maley said was true – 'It's not the man's creed or nationality that counts; it's the man himself.'

A visit to Celtic Park on matchday reveals all sorts from fresh-faced youngsters bedecked in green to wizened old men who talk about Charlie Tully and Willie Fernie. There is the

Green Brigade with their occasionally revolutionary and subversive sentiments in the North-East corner, the hosts of mothers and children, the staid habitués of the South Stand whom advancing years has compelled this author to join, the physically handicapped, the ex-players, the occasional personality – politician perhaps or television entertainer, actor, sportsman or -woman distinguished in snooker, swimming or golf. Glance at the provenance of the buses in the Bus Park – Elgin, Northampton, Donegal, Teesside, for example – it's not unlike the description of 'far-summoned allies' of ancient Troy in Homer's *Iliad*. They all have one thing in common – they love 'the' Celtic, the definite article used unselfconsciously and deliberately. It is to such people that this book is dedicated.

My thanks are due to my friends like Tom Campbell, Marie Rowan, George Sheridan, Dan Leslie, Mark O'Brien, Craig McAughtrie and many others who have encouraged me and shared their love for 'the' Celtic.

This book does not claim to be comprehensive. It is a hotch-potch, an amalgam whimsically selected to entertain and hopefully to bring a smile to the faces of the support as Celtic face a new era. At the time of writing, our greatest rivals are seriously and perhaps permanently crippled. They almost left us altogether and may yet do so. On the surface, this sounds good for Celtic, but the new era will bring fresh challenges and fresh problems, and will impose great demands on the support and the players.

But I have little doubt that Celtic will rise to it. Celtic are, after all, a very special club. To those who are not yet imbued with the Celtic spirit, I say one thing – Join us!

Enjoy this book!

David Potter, August 2012

RECORD SCORE

Celtic beat Dundee 11–0 at Parkhead on 26 October 1895 in the Scottish League in what is still a Celtic record score for a competitive match, but one should not really read too much into it. The pitch was frankly unplayable after heavy overnight snow and Dundee were very critical of referee Mr J. Baillie's decision to let the game go ahead. Dundee had three players injured and in the second half took the field with only nine men, but by this time the score was already 6–0 to Celtic, who had to change their strips because the green and white vertical stripes clashed with the blue and white vertical of Dundee. Accounts of who scored all the goals vary, but the general consensus seems to be that Johnny Madden scored 3, Jimmy Blessington 2, Barney Battles 2, Allan Martin 2, James Kelly 1 and Willie Ferguson 1.

SCOTTISH CUP

This competition is, not without cause, looked upon as Celtic's favourite competition, for they have won it on 35 occasions between 1892 and 2011, and that is twice more than Rangers. Celtic's love affair with the competition started as early as their first season when they reached the final in 1889 only to lose to Third Lanark. It is often felt that there is nothing better than Hampden in the sun on a warm day in April or May for those who wish to see quintessential Celtic football. Certainly there have been many epic Scottish Cup finals in the past – 1904, 1925, 1931, 1965, 1985, 1988 – all of which have been much celebrated in Celtic folklore. Curiously Celtic have never done something that Rangers, Aberdeen, Queen's Park and Vale of Leven have all done and that is win the trophy three years in a row. Of the three hat-tricks scored in Scottish Cup finals, the first two were scored by Celtic players – Jimmy Quinn in 1904 and Dixie Deans in 1972. Celtic's 35 successful Scottish Cup finals have been as follows:

Celtic 5–1 Queen's Park, Ibrox, 9 April 1892

Campbell (2), McMahon (2), own goal

Originally scheduled for 12 March but declared a friendly after crowd encroachment, this was Celtic's first Scottish Cup win and the victory that really put them on the map, causing outlandish scenes of joy in the East End.

Celtic 2–0 Rangers, Second Hampden, 22 April 1899

McMahon, Hodge

A victory which was all the more creditable as Rangers had been league champions with a 100 per cent record.

Celtic 4–3 Queen's Park, Ibrox, 14 April 1900

Divers (2), McMahon, Bell

Commonly referred to as the 'hurricane' final, this game saw Celtic go in at half time with a 3–1 lead. Despite facing the strong wind in the second half, it was Celtic who scored the crucial fourth goal early in the period and after Queen's Park scored two, they held out to register their third cup final victory.

Celtic 3–2 Rangers, Hampden, 16 April 1904

Quinn (3)

This is the game which made Jimmy Quinn. Celtic were two down, but Quinn levelled before half time then scored the winner in the second half to register the first ever Scottish Cup final hat-trick.

Celtic 3–0 Hearts, Hampden, 20 April 1907

Somers (2), Orr (penalty)

Celtic became the first team to win the Scottish League and the Scottish Cup in the same year. Hearts were handicapped by the absence through injury of Charlie Thomson. This was the beginning of Hearts' trophy famine of 50 years and also the start of their perpetual and irrational hatred and complex about Celtic.

Celtic 5–1 St Mirren, Hampden, 18 April 1908

Bennett (2), Hamilton, Somers, Quinn

It would have taken a great team to beat this all-conquering Celtic side, and the Buddies were not that. Jimmy McMenemy controlled the game from start to finish.

Celtic 2–0 Hamilton (after 0–0 draw), Ibrox, 15 April 1911

Quinn, McAteer

By no means a vintage Celtic side, but a great day for the village of Croy which supplied three men for Celtic – Jimmy Quinn, Andy McAtee and Tommy McAteer.

Celtic 2–0 Clyde, Ibrox, 6 April 1912

McMenemy, Gallacher

Another windy final and Patsy Gallacher marked his first cup final with a goal.

Celtic 4–1 Hibs (after 0–0 draw), Ibrox, 16 April 1914

McColl (2), Browning (2)

A superb performance by Celtic in the 'Irish' Cup final on this Thursday evening. Patsy Gallacher played magnificently.

Celtic 1–0 Hibs, Hampden, 31 March 1923

Cassidy

A poorish Celtic side had to work hard for this narrow victory, but Joe Cassidy's goal was the difference.

Celtic 2–1 Dundee, Hampden, 11 April 1925

Gallacher, McGrory

Patsy Gallacher's famous goal in this final was scored with the ball wedged between his feet as he somersaulted into the net. Young McGrory scored the winner with a stereotypical diving header.

Celtic 3–1 East Fife, Hampden, 16 April 1927

McLean, Connolly, own goal

Second Division East Fife did well to reach the final but were outclassed by Celtic. Tommy McInally clowned throughout and deliberately missed chances so as not to embarrass the Fifers. This was the first cup final to be broadcast on the radio and it was listened to in ice cream parlours in Methil.

Celtic 4–2 Motherwell (after 2–2 draw), Hampden, 15 April 1931

McGrory (2), R. Thomson (2)

A great performance after being lucky to earn a replay, yet it is the first game that is the more famous. Celtic were now able to take the Scottish Cup with them on tour to America.

Celtic 1–0 Motherwell, Hampden, 15 April 1933

McGrory

A dull game on a dull day with only Jimmy McGrory's tap-in separating the sides.

Celtic 2–1 Aberdeen, Hampden, 24 April 1937

Crum, Buchan

Hampden's record crowd for a Scottish Cup final (with a lot more inside than the 147,365 officially given) saw a tight game with Celtic emerging victorious.

Celtic 1–0 Motherwell, Hampden, 21 April 1951

McPhail

John McPhail's first-half goal was enough to separate the teams and give Celtic their first piece of silverware since before the Second World War.

Celtic 2–1 Aberdeen, Hampden, 24 April 1954

own goal, Fallon

Celtic's hard-earned victory over a spirited Dons side saw the first league and cup double for 40 years.

Celtic 3–2 Dunfermline, Hampden, 24 April 1965

Auld (2), McNeill

A truly epic occasion as Celtic with Jock Stein now at the helm ending their trophy famine in glorious style, after twice being behind.

Celtic 2–0 Aberdeen, Hampden, 29 April 1967

Wallace (2)

The all-conquering Celtic side had just become the first British side to reach a European Cup final on the previous Tuesday, and Wallace's two goals on either side of half time were enough to do the trick.

Celtic 4–0 Rangers, Hampden, 26 April 1969

McNeill, Lennox, Connelly, Chalmers

Celtic completed a domestic treble with this comprehensive rout of Rangers.

Celtic 2–1 Rangers (after 1–1 draw), Hampden, 12 May 1971

Macari, Hood (penalty)

A good win for Celtic on the Wednesday night after a late goal on the Saturday had given Rangers an undeserved replay. George Connelly was superb.

Celtic 6–1 Hibs, Hampden, 6 May 1972

Deans (3), Macari (2), McNeill

A great victory for Celtic with Dixie Deans equalling the feat of Jimmy Quinn in 1904 with a cup final hat-trick, one of them celebrated with a somersault.

Celtic 3–0 Dundee United, Hampden, 4 May 1974

Hood, Murray, Deans

Dundee United's first Scottish Cup final appearance and they were defeated by a Celtic team which had possibly passed its best, but was still too good for anyone in Scotland.

Celtic 3–1 Airdrie, Hampden, 3 May 1975

Wilson (2), P. McCluskey

Billy McNeill announced his retirement after this game. A Celtic victory was all the more essential because Rangers had won the league for the first time in a decade.

Celtic 1–0 Rangers, Hampden, 7 May 1977

Lynch (penalty)

A miserable rainy day and the first time that the Scottish Cup final had been televised live for twenty years. Celtic's goal came from a disputed penalty, but they were the better team in any case.

Celtic 1–0 Rangers (after extra time), Hampden, 10 May 1980

G. McCluskey

A reasonable game of football overshadowed by the Hampden Riot afterwards as idiots from either side battled it out on the field after the game to the undisguised delight of the media.

Celtic 2–1 Dundee United, Hampden, 18 May 1985

Provan, McGarvey

A great Celtic comeback in the last 15 minutes over a stuffy Dundee United defence was much needed to give the support and manager Davie Hay something to cheer about after a dreadful season.

Celtic 2–1 Dundee United, Hampden, 14 May 1988

McAvennie (2)

Almost a carbon copy of 1985, but Billy McNeill was now the manager and this victory gave Celtic the double of league and cup in their centenary season.

Celtic 1–0 Rangers, Hampden, 20 May 1989

Miller

Joe Miller scored the only goal of this Cup final just before half time.

Celtic 1–0 Airdrie, Hampden, 27 May 1995

van Hooijdonk

A poorish game but Celtic's early goal was enough to give manager Tommy Burns the only trophy of his managerial career.

Celtic 3–0 Hibs, Hampden, 26 May 2001

McNamara, Larsson (2, 1 a penalty)

This game over an outclassed Hibs side sealed a treble in Martin O'Neill's first season in charge.

Celtic 3–1 Dunfermline, Hampden, 22 May 2004

Larsson (2), Petrov

A good Celtic comeback after a dodgy Dunfermline goal in the first half in what was Henrik Larsson's last competitive game for the club.

Celtic 1–0 Dundee United, Hampden, 28 May 2005

Thompson

Celtic had disappointed their fans by throwing away the SPL at Motherwell the previous week in what became known as Black Sunday, and then Martin O'Neill announced his resignation to look after his ill wife. Not the greatest ever Celtic performance on a wet and misty day, but a welcome win nevertheless.

Celtic 1–0 Dunfermline, Hampden, 26 May 2007

Perrier-Doumbé

A poor game but the late goal from the unlikely source of Cameroon international Jean-Joël Perrier-Doumbé was enough to do the trick for Gordon Strachan.

Celtic 3–0 Motherwell, Hampden, 21 May 2011

Ki, Wilson, Mulgrew

A businesslike performance from Celtic to give Neil Lennon his first honour after the SPL had been lost in a strange performance at Inverness.

RESCUED FROM DROWNING

A brave piece of swimming by a Scottish tourist which saved an Irish girl from drowning one day on Lough Gill, County Sligo, in the summer of 1947 had important consequences for Celtic. The Scottish holidaymaker was Joseph McMenemy, son of the great 'Napoleon' and the local girl was Lily Fallon. Naturally the hero was invited back to the Fallon household for tea, and conversation turned of course to Glasgow Celtic to the particular interest of Lily's brother Sean, a talented player for some local teams. In 1950, Sean Fallon signed for Celtic, and then contributed hugely to the club for the next sixty years.

GEORGE WHITEHEAD

This man does not figure prominently in histories of Celtic, yet he has a 100 per cent record of winning every game he played in, and of scoring against Rangers at Ibrox. It was autumn 1913 and Celtic were struggling with injuries to McMenemy and Quinn, while George Whitehead was struggling to find a place in the Hearts first team. He was therefore borrowed, played a brilliant seven games at centre forward beside Sniper McColl and Patsy Gallacher, but the club them let him return to Hearts – a decision that was not all that popular with the support. Hearts then promptly sold him to Motherwell! During the First World War, he served in the Royal Navy, was torpedoed twice and happily survived!

PENALTIES!

Celtic played in an astonishing game at East Fife on 17 February 1973. East Fife had fought their way back into the old First Division after many years in the Second Division, and their ground at Bayview was packed with 11,000 spectators. The game ended 2–2 with Celtic earning their draw with a late goal from Dixie Deans who had also scored their first – but that was not the whole story. Celtic had been awarded two penalties (both justified, of course!) and three separate players – Bobby Murdoch, Harry Hood (with the retake of Murdoch's) and Kenny Dalglish – had missed them! East Fife were more grateful – when they were awarded a penalty, they took it and scored. Even after Deans' late equaliser in the 88th minute, there was a late appeal for a penalty, but most fans were delighted and relieved when referee George Smith of Edinburgh said 'No'.

THE TROOPER

Joe Cassidy signed for Celtic in 1913, but the First World War delayed his career until the 1920s. He served in the Black Watch and won a Military Medal in the closing days of the conflict in November 1918. He was back in time to play in the New Year's Day game of 1919, but it was the following season before he was able to resume his career in earnest.

He won his spurs on New Year's Day 1921 at Ibrox when his two goals sent the faithful into raptures and had the fans declaring that he was the new Jimmy Quinn. Indeed he was big and strong and had the added advantage of being good-looking as well, thus winning the hearts of so many female fans. He was originally an inside left, but Tommy McInally's temporary departure in 1922 opened the door for him as a centre forward.

His *annus mirabilis* was certainly 1923 when he rescued a dreadful season by scoring 11 goals in the triumphant Scottish Cup campaign, scoring in every game except one (and even in that one, he hit the post!). Before the crowd had settled, he grabbed a goal in the first minute against Motherwell in the semi-final, and the only goal of the game with a header against Hibs in the final, which brought the Scottish Cup to Parkhead for the tenth time overall and for the first time since the war.

He was unfairly scapegoated for the awful 1923/24 season and allowed to go to Bolton Wanderers in summer 1924, but not before he had played his part in grooming the young McGrory to stardom. He never settled in England and returned to Dundee but he was always Joe Cassidy of Celtic. He later went to Ireland and won an Irish Cup medal with Ballymena in 1929. He won four caps for Scotland.

A HAMMERING

It was just as well that the Scottish Cup had been won the week before, because Celtic chose the night of Friday 30 April 1937 to play one of their worst ever games as they went down 8–0 to Motherwell at Fir Park. No excuse was possible, other than that the game was totally meaningless and that they were just about to embark on the overnight sleeper to London to see the English FA Cup final between Sunderland and Preston North End. Nevertheless it was a distressing experience for the many Celtic fans in the crowd.

THE TRAGEDY OF KENNY DALGLISH

It is sad that Kenny Dalglish is so much associated with Liverpool rather than Celtic, for so much of his career with Celtic was superb and much reminisced about by those fortunate enough to have seen him play. Even at the interval of thirty-five years since his departure to Liverpool, it is hard to analyse one's own feelings and to refrain from using words like 'tragedy' in the context of the loss of Kenny Dalglish.

Kenny joined Celtic in the momentous summer of 1967, was farmed out to Cumbernauld United but then played his debut in 1968. He played only occasionally for the first team until he really broke through in 1971, famously scoring a penalty against Rangers at Ibrox on the opening day of that season – but not before he had bent down to tie his lace first!

Kenny was one of the 'Quality Street Kids', those specially reared to replace the now-ageing Lisbon Lions, and the team was good enough to reach two European Cup semi-finals in 1972 and 1974. It was fairly obvious from an early stage that Dalglish was a special player with the ability to distribute the ball, to control play and to take a great goal himself. He very soon became a hero with the fans, and it was no great surprise when he was awarded his first Scottish cap against Belgium at Pittodrie in November 1971, a matter of months after breaking into the Celtic team.

He played a great part in Celtic's sustained success in the early 1970s, an era in which they could win whatever they wanted except the Scottish League Cup final – but it was Dalglish who scored Celtic's only goal in the Partick Thistle shocker of October 1971.

He was competent enough without being outstanding for Scotland in the 1974 World Cup in West Germany, but his form seemed to take a slight dip at the start of the 1974/75 season. The league was lost that season (although both cups were won, including the elusive League Cup) and Kenny made noises about wanting a transfer before being bought off with the captaincy for the difficult and fruitless season of 1975/76 when Jock Stein was in hospital recovering from a car accident. It was no accident that Stein's return and Dalglish's fine form happened at the same time, for 1976/77 was a great season for the club with Dalglish leading Celtic to a league and cup double.

It would be wrong to say that Dalglish was always universally popular with the fans who seemed to pick on him when the team had a bad day, but men like John Rafferty in the *Scotsman* would frequently single him out as being 'worth the admission money on his own,' and he was never 'rested' or 'dropped'. He was always the consummate professional and a wonderful role model for youngsters.

What went on behind the scenes in his relationship with Jock Stein we will never know, but August 1977 saw him leave for Liverpool. Celtic were devastated, the fans were stunned, and Stein seemed to suffer a mini-nervous breakdown where his judgement in other matters seemed to leave him as well. Celtic had a shocker of a season (not helped by the obvious success of Dalglish and Liverpool) and it took them a good two years to recover.

He was involved with the club in the terrible 1999/2000 season and must take a share of the blame for the Inverness Caledonian Thistle fiasco, but he is worthy of a little praise for his role as caretaker-manager in the capture of the Scottish League Cup in March 2000. It was a poor final played between two terrible teams (Celtic and Aberdeen) but Celtic did win through, and it put a brief smile on our faces.

FLOODLIGHTS

Celtic were on the slow side about installing floodlights, failing to see the benefits that could accrue from midweek European football. But the lights were generally believed to be of a high standard and the pylons became a landmark over the east end of Glasgow for many years. They were officially opened on Monday 12 October 1959 in a game against Wolverhampton Wanderers, champions of England for the last two years. Wolves won 2–0. It was unfortunate that Willie Fernie, Bobby Collins and Bobby Evans all left the club at about the same time and supporters found it hard to resist the conclusion that the sale of these excellent players paid for the floodlights.

DZIEKANOWSKI, AITKENOFFSKI AND MILLERONANDOFFSKI

It was said that Celtic had three Polish players in the Scottish League Cup final of 20 September 1989. It was a dreadful game in which Celtic lost 1–0 to Aberdeen to a goal from Ian Cameron. Manager Billy McNeill took off Steve Fulton and put on Joe Miller, but Joe failed to do what McNeill told him to do and had to be himself substituted by Andy Walker for refusing, presumably, to follow McNeill's instructions. This was greeted with anger from the Celtic support, laughter from the Aberdeen support (not least because Miller was an ex-Aberdeen player) and incredulity from the radio commentators and journalists. Thing got a lot worse for

Celtic when Roy Aitken was sent off for two yellow cards, and even star man Dariusz Dziekanowski (commonly known as Jackie) could do little about it. Hence the three Poles – Dziekanowski, Aitkenoffski and Milleronandoffski.

'IS IT TRUE WHAT THEY SAY ABOUT DIXIE?'

John Deans' career was going nowhere fast in autumn 1971. He was playing for Motherwell, or rather he wasn't, for he was in the middle of a six-week suspension when Stein surprised the world by offering £17,500 for him. This all happened in the aftermath of Celtic's dreadful League Cup final defeat at the hands of Partick Thistle, and Stein was clearly making a point to some of his players who, he felt, had let him down. Yet the chunky under-performing Deans with a bad disciplinary record did not seem to be the man for the job. Some Celtic supporters remembered the debut day of Willie Wallace at Parkhead in December 1966 when Motherwell had been the opposition and Deans had been sent off!

But Deans duly served the suspension, and scored in his debut against Partick Thistle in late November, thereafter finding the net with a certain frequency and teaming-up well with the precociously talented Kenny Dalglish as Celtic marched inexorably towards their record-breaking seventh league championship in a row. But the events of spring 1972 were characterised by Dixie Deans. Celtic might have reached the European Cup final but Deans was the unlucky man who missed a penalty in the shoot-out. This would have shattered lesser men, but Stein and the fans kept faith with him, and on 6 May in the Scottish Cup final against the not inconsiderable opposition of Eddie Turnbull's Hibs, he scored the hat-trick which put him on the same level as Jimmy Quinn, the only other man to score a hat-trick in a Scottish Cup final.

Further success followed with a league medal in 1973, won in breathtaking circumstances on the last day at Easter Road with two goals from Dixie Deans, and then in 1974 a league and cup double with Deans again scoring in the Scottish Cup final against the overawed Dundee United. In 1972/73 and 1973/74 Celtic lost the League Cup finals to Hibs and Dundee and it is not without significance that Deans was absent from both those line-ups. But he did play in the League Cup final of 1974/75, and how! He scored a hat-trick in the 6–3 victory, thus becoming the only man ever to score a hat-trick in each of Scotland's domestic cup finals.

Celtic fans have always loved a goalscorer, especially one with the personality and lion heart of Dixie Deans, given that nickname in conscious imitation of Dixie Dean of Everton in the 1920s. Deans was not a Celt by background. He claims he was a St Mirren supporter (although others mention Rangers in this context), but he very soon was adopted by Celtic fans as one of their own. His relationship with Stein was by no means always cordial, but Stein managed to bring out the best in him and it was no coincidence that in the 1975/76 season when Stein was in hospital following his car accident, Deans' form was patchy and indifferent. By summer 1976 he had moved on to Coventry. It was a pity that he had not come to Celtic a little earlier in his career.

He remains an ever cheerful member of the Celtic family, always ready to talk to supporters, and was seen at the Celtic end of Hampden with his suit and green tie before the 2011 Scottish Cup final. When reminded about his hat-trick in

1972, and told that that feat put him in the same bracket as Jimmy Quinn, he smiled and said 'Aye, but I did it twice!' – not technically true because one was a Scottish League Cup final, but let's not quibble!

ZERO TO HERO

The literati call it 'peripeteia' or reversal of fortunes. Seldom can there have been such a total change in two successive Scottish Cup finals as there was for Roy Aitken between 1984 and 1985. In 1984 Celtic were a goal down to Aberdeen (a goal which should have been disallowed) when Roy tackled (future Celt) Mark McGhee. McGhee went down and (future Celtic manager) Gordon Strachan was seen to influence referee Bob Valentine and to persuade him to send (future Aberdeen manager) Roy Atiken off. Ten-man Celtic then fought like tigers, earned a late equaliser, but went down in extra time to a goal scored by Mark McGhee, apparently having recovered from Aitken's challenge. Hell could not be so terrible as 19 May 1984 was for Roy Aitken.

But then fast forward to 18 May 1985 with the stuffy, defence-minded Dundee United 1–0 up and time running out for Celtic. Then manager Davie Hay brings off Paul McStay, puts on defender Pierce O'Leary for one of his rare outings and puts Roy Aitken into midfield. The effect is instantaneous. Roy takes hold of the game 'by the scruff of the neck' and Celtic win 2–1. Roy is the hero of the hour!

THE REDOUBTABLE
JIMMY DELANEY

Jimmy Delaney is unique in world football history in that he has won cup winners' medals in three different countries – Celtic in 1937, Manchester United in 1948 and Derry City in 1954. It was a pity that the Second World War got in the way, otherwise there might have been a lot more! But if that were not enough to be going on with, he also managed to score two goals for Scotland against Germany at Ibrox in 1936, thereby thoroughly upsetting the gentleman with the moustache and the funny salute in Berlin who was already struggling to cope with Jesse Owens spoiling his Olympics! Then at the end of the war, it was 'Jaydee' (as he was called) who scored the goal in the Victory International of 1946 at Hampden which beat England, and sent football-starved Scotland into untold ecstasy.

THE STRANGEST SENDING OFF
OF THEM ALL

Johnny Doyle was famously sent off in the game in 1979 when 'ten men won the league'. He possibly deserved that one, but on an earlier occasion he was definitely the victim of an injustice and one that had more than a little touch of farce about it. It happened on 20 August 1977 at Somerset Park, funnily enough the home of Doyle's previous club, Ayr United. Johnny hit the ball at full power and it hit the unfortunate referee Bob Cuthill full in the face. The game was immediately stopped and the referee was given attention from Ayr's trainer. Once he recovered (or seemed to), he summoned Doyle and, to the astonishment and horror of all concerned, ordered Doyle off the field! The referee was obviously stunned and could not really be blamed but it was a mystery why one or other of the linesmen did not intervene. Doyle ran off the field in tears to be comforted by Jock Stein. The ordering off was later rescinded and no suspension given, but nothing could be done about the result which remained Ayr United 2–1 Celtic. Coming as this did only ten days after the Dalglish transfer, it was another massive blow to the beleaguered Celtic support.

FORGOTTEN BOOTS

This unfortunate happening occurred to John Divers at the start of the 1962/63 season. It was the first day of the season, a bright lovely August day and a big crowd was expected at Celtic Park to see Hearts. John set out in his car to drive to the ground, then realised that his boots would not be at Celtic Park because he had been playing in a Charity friendly at Hampden on the previous Wednesday night and had taken his boots home. So he turned back to get them but was then caught up in traffic and turned up late for the game. His place was given to Charlie Gallagher, and Celtic, with Bobby Murdoch playing his debut, beat Hearts 3–1. The team had played so well that the formation was retained and Divers remained out of the team for all the League Cup sectional matches. It was tight section involving Hearts and the two Dundee teams. Celtic failed to qualify in heart-breaking circumstances by the narrowest of margins and it is a moot point and much argued by historians whether the presence of the experienced Divers might have made a difference. Life might have been different if John had remembered his boots or even continued driving to Celtic Park and borrowed someone else's.

THE LOST CELT

Few Celtic players have caused more distress than Pat Crerand. A brilliant right-half who lit up the early 1960s, he was the one of the few undeniably world class players at Celtic Park at the time. But Pat became disillusioned with the lack of success at Parkhead, had an argument with a member of the coaching staff at half time at Ibrox on New Year's Day 1963 after which the team went on to lose heavily, then in the middle of the big freeze of February 1963 Crerand was transferred to Manchester United where he became part of Matt Busby's great side. For Celtic supporters, the pain was intense.

BAIRD'S BAR

This is by no means the only Celtic bar in the Gallowgate but it is the most famous, not least because Kenny Dalglish, when interim manager in 2000, once decided to hold his Friday press conference there. It is the only bar in which the author has ever been showered with champagne as he walked in the door (this was the night that Celtic won the League Cup in March 2009). It has loads of Celtic memorabilia on the walls and is well worth a visit.

THE GREATEST OF THEM ALL?

Although an Irishman born in Ramelton, County Donegal, Patsy Gallacher lived most of his life in Scotland and was, in the opinion of most who were alive at the time, the greatest player of them all. He joined Celtic from Clydebank Juniors and made his debut for Celtic in December 1911, playing for them until 1926 when he joined Falkirk, for whom he played until 1932.

Less than six months after his debut, Patsy had won a Scottish Cup medal, scoring in the 1912 final against Clyde, and by 1914 he was the inspirational mainstay of the great team which won the Scottish league and cup double. The First World War meant that Patsy had to get a job in John Brown's Shipyard where he was once fined and suspended from playing for Celtic for 'bad-timekeeping', but this did not stop him playing phenomenal football and becoming 'the most talked about man in the trenches'.

He is best remembered for the famous goal that he scored (he somersaulted into the net with the ball wedged between his legs) in the Scottish Cup final against Dundee in 1925, and the goal that he scored against Hibs at Easter Road in September 1921 when he ran all the way from the centre after Hibs had scored, to score without any other player touching the ball. He played eleven times for Ireland, including once for the Irish Free State.

He was also involved in the licensing trade and ran the International Bar in Clydebank. His son Willie played for Celtic and his other son Tommy played for Dundee, and his grandson Kevin played for a number of clubs and earned 53 caps for Scotland.

DAVIE McLEAN

This man actually scored more goals than Jimmy McGrory, but as a great deal of them were scored for Forfar Athletic in the Second Division, they are not considered as important. He played for Celtic for a brief spell between 1907 and 1909, but suffered for two reasons. One was that he was a centre forward at the same time as Jimmy Quinn, and the other was that he was less prepared than some to put up with the bullying of Maley. But he had two great moments for Celtic – one was when, as a 17-year-old, he scored the goal which won the Glasgow Cup final replay of 1907 with a 'well-judged shot of power' after which he was 'smothered by the congratulations of his team mates,' and the other time was when Celtic needed to play 12 games in 8 days to win the Scottish League in 1909. Injuries compelled the use of fringe players and McLean was heavily employed in that glorious fortnight.

But he had not played enough games to win a League medal, and the following autumn he was on his way, playing for Preston North End, Sheffield Wednesday, Forfar Athletic, Third Lanark, Rangers, Bradford Park Avenue, Dundee and Forfar Athletic again. He won a Scotland cap in 1912 in a 1–1 draw against England, and on two occasions he returned to haunt Celtic – one was when he scored a hat-trick for Third Lanark against Celtic in 1918 in a game which effectively cost Celtic the league championship, and the other was when he scored for Dundee in the 1925 Scottish Cup final – but on this occasion Patsy Gallacher and Jimmy McGrory famously repaired the damage.

In latter years he retained his love for the club, having made his peace with Maley, and until his death in 1967 was a frequent guest of the club on big occasions, often with his brother George who had also played professional football, and his great friend Jimmy McMenemy.

CELTIC'S WAR HEROES

Celtic won the Scottish League four years in a row between 1914 and 1917. As a result, they were often the butt of sneers of 'war-dodging' in that manager Willie Maley was able to find war-related jobs for his excellent side, so that they were always available to play for Celtic. This charge was unfair, for the men concerned did valuable jobs in the shipyards and the mines, and in any case takes no account of the Celtic players who were killed – Peter Johnstone, Leigh Roose, Donnie McLeod, Patrick Slavin, Archie McMillan, Robert Craig and John McLaughlin nor indeed Willie Angus who won the Victoria Cross and survived the war as one of the war-blinded.

INVERNESS CALEDONIAN THISTLE

The night of 8 February 2000 is like a stake driven through the heart of every Celtic supporter, but it was only the beginning, as it were, for Celtic also managed to throw away the Scottish Cup there in 2003 and the SPL in 2011. But the events of 2000 led to the 'Super Caley go ballistic, Celtic are atrocious' headline and the departure of John Barnes from his ill-fated tenure as Celtic manager. It might all have been different if the game had been played on its original date of 29 January but it had been postponed because of high winds and the fear of bits being blown off the Parkhead stands. As it was, Celtic had a shocking game against Hearts at Parkhead on 5 February in which they were two goals up but managed to lose 3–2, and protests were heard against John Barnes, for Celtic were now 10 points behind Rangers and virtually out of contention for the SPL.

Celtic then went into this Scottish Cup game against Inverness with several players clearly unhappy with their manager and their team-mates, and the traditional Celtic team spirit was conspicuous by its absence. The 3–1 defeat was totally deserved. Reports of fisticuffs in the dressing room were not denied, and it was one of the worst nights in Celtic's history. John Barnes was dismissed soon afterwards.

DIRECT FROM A CORNER KICK – TWICE!

A goal can be scored direct from a corner kick, but it is not usual, for it is a difficult feat. On 21 February 1953 at Brockville, Falkirk, with Celtic behind in a Scottish Cup tie, Charlie Tully scored direct from a corner kick – or so he thought. The linesman, however, flagged for an infringement in that the ball had not been placed properly in the arc. The crowd were furious, but Charlie calmly took the ball for the retake and politely asked the linesman to place the ball for him. The official did so, and Tully swung the ball in and scored again! This time the goal was allowed and crush barriers collapsed under the pressure of the crowd surging forward. Celtic would eventually win the game 3–2.

DUN

James 'Dun' Hay was one of Celtic's greatest ever players. His record as captain of the great six league championships in a row team from 1905 to 1910 speaks for itself, as well as the very fact that he was part of the immortal triumvirate of Young, Loney and Hay, who are still talked about over a century after their apogee. Not a tall man, but with broad shoulders and totally courageous and committed, James Hay was a visionary player in a team which was, without much doubt, the best in the world at the time.

THE JUNGLE

The 'Jungle' was a hideous barn-like structure which stood on the north side of the ground from 1907 until 1966, then it was replaced by a better enclosure which lasted until the ground was redeveloped in 1994 (seating was installed for the 1993/94 season). No-one seems to know why the name 'Jungle' was coined, but it is believed to owe its genesis to ex-servicemen returning in 1945 from Burma and comparing the enclosure unfavourably to what they had experienced in the Far East! Not only was the Jungle ugly, the cover provided did not reach the front of the terracing and there were also holes in the roof which grew progressively larger season by season. Little was ever done to repair the damage until it was at last demolished in 1966. The Jungle, however, had a certain amount of character and saw some great football players in its time.

HANDS ACROSS THE ATLANTIC

Celtic have had some great goalkeepers, but very few have been as good as the Canadian Joe Kennaway. Joe first crossed Celtic's path on the summer tour of North America in 1931 when he played brilliantly for a team called Fall River. A month or two later came the tragic death of John Thomson, and in a desperate search for his successor, someone remembered James [sic] Kennaway and he was summoned across the Atlantic. It was a tremendous leap of faith for both Kennaway and for Celtic, but he arrived in time to play his first game on 31 October 1931.

Celtic were going through a bad spell, suffering all sorts of trauma in the wake of John Thomson's death, but very soon supporters found a hero in the cheery and athletic Canadian who developed a bond of affection and affinity with the support. It was soon seen that he was in the Thomson mould of being lithe and agile, never afraid to come out and command the penalty area, and with large hands which he could use to fist the ball away some distance from the danger area.

He had already played for Canada, and on 29 November 1933 became the first ever goalkeeper to play for two countries when he won a cap for Scotland against Austria and performed well in a 2–2 draw. He should have played against Wales at Cardiff a month earlier, but was ill and had to withdraw.

By this time he had already won a Scottish Cup medal in a 1–0 win over Motherwell. This was a poor final, lightened only by McGrory's goal and some fine goalkeeping from Kennaway including one shot from George Stevenson which he dived to punch away. For a while, it seemed that this was to be the only honour that Kennaway would win, but suddenly in about 1935, Celtic clicked and playing some superb football began to win the honours again. A great deal of this was due to the forward play of the two Jimmies (Delaney and McGrory) but the defence was also sound with Kennaway developing a fine understanding with centre-half Willie Lyon.

The Empire Exhibition Trophy was not won without a few hairy moments, especially in the quarter-final when the injury-hit Celtic had their backs to the wall against the strong Sunderland side before eventually winning through, and in the final itself Celtic were more than once heavily dependent on the shrewd positional sense of Joe Kennaway, particularly in the last desperate minutes when the mighty Everton side threw everything at them.

Suffering from rheumatism and now 34, Kennaway called it a day soon after war was declared in 1939 and returned to his native Canada, where he died 30 years later in 1969. He remains one of Celtic's best ever goalkeepers.

FRANK AND NUMBER NINE

Supporters tore their hair out at the thought of Frank Haffey – on his day a brilliant goalkeeper, other times capable of some tremendous howlers. He played twice for Scotland against England, saving a penalty at Hampden in 1960 but being the man who had to fish the ball out of the net nine times at Wembley the following year. Not all the goals were Frank's fault – but some of them were, and poor Frank had to shoulder far more of the blame than he should have.

He played in two Scottish Cup finals in 1961 and 1963, both of which went to replays. In 1961, only a matter of ten days after the Wembley fiasco, Frank gave away the goal which effectively won the cup for Dunfermline, but in the first game in 1963, he gave a tremendous performance denying Rangers again and again and earning newspaper headlines like 'Franktastic', 'Haffey the Hero' and 'Fantastic Frank'.

But then in October 1963, the number nine came into his life again. It was 26 October and although everyone at Parkhead was aware that Rangers were winning the League Cup a little over a mile away at Hampden, the Celtic team, having recovered from their awful start to the season, delighted their fans by putting nine past Airdrie. It was 9–0 and late in the game, Celtic were awarded a penalty that they scarcely needed. Frank was invited to do the deed and put Celtic into double figures. Out of respect for his fellow goalkeeper Roddy McKenzie, he missed!

Frank also fancied himself as a singer with 'The Dear Little Shamrock' and 'Slattery's Mounted Fut', but later emigrated to Australia like 'The Wild Colonial Boy'!

NO ROAD THIS WAY

Willie Loney was a powerful centre-half, called, not without cause, 'The Obliterator' for the way in which he could break up opposition attacks, simply by reading a situation and being in the right place to deal with it. He was also called 'No Road This Way'.

Yet he was an unlucky player as well. A broken arm kept him out for a large part of the 1906/07 season and another injury prevented him playing in the latter part of the 1909 season and may have indirectly caused the Hampden riot for Loney would surely have stopped Rangers from scoring in both the final and its replay in a way that the young Joe Dodds (as yet inexperienced and a far better left-back than a centre-half) didn't.

Thirty-three is a surprising amount of goals for a centre-half to score, but we must remember that many teams, including Celtic, played the attacking centre-half game, and there was the additional factor that Loney would often change places with his great friend Jimmy Quinn to deceive the opposition, for they both shared the same massive build.

He arrived from Denny at the turn of the century, was tried now and again at right-half (he played there in what is sometimes called the 'Coronation Cup Final' of 1902) before settling down at centre-half with Jimmy Young and Jimmy Hay on either side of him to form the most famous half-back line in Celtic's history.

It is surprising that he was capped only twice for Scotland, but his habit of being injured in the spring (1907, 1909 and 1911) when internationals were played did not help and in any case, Scotland had fine centre-halves in Charlie Thomson of Hearts and Sunderland and Alex Raisbeck of Liverpool. It remains a pity that Loney never played against England, but he did play in the fine 3–2 win for the Scottish League over the English League at Ewood Park in February 1910.

He left in 1913 to play for Motherwell, Partick Thistle and Clydebank before finally retiring in 1917.

CELTIC PARK

Celtic Park has existed on the same site since 1892 (the original Celtic Park which was in use from 1888 until 1892 lay a few hundred yards to the east of the present ground). The first game played on the current Celtic Park was on 20 August 1892 when Celtic beat Renton 4–3 with Johnny Campbell scoring all four goals. Johnny Madden had a less happy day, for he and McQuilkie of Renton were 'invited to retire' (i.e. sent off) for fighting.

THERE'S SURELY NO DENYIN', WI' OOR CAPTAIN WILLIE LYON

Willie Lyon was anything but a Celt in background, ethnicity or even (in his early days) inclination. He was an Englishman whose family had moved to Scotland and he found himself playing for Queen's Park and indeed had a few jousts with Celtic between 1933 and 1935 before he joined the club.

His transfer to Celtic in 1935 was unusual in that Celtic did not usually buy many players from anyone, and certainly not Queen's Park, a club that Celtic supporters looked upon with suspicion for their perceived middle-class base. But Celtic needed a centre-half now that Jimmy McStay had gone. Malky MacDonald had been tried in that position but was a different kind of player, and the tall, rangy and mobile Lyon seemed a good idea. Most of the credit for this decision, one feels, must go to the newly appointed trainer Jimmy McMenemy who had played alongside Willie Loney and Alec McNair and knew what a good defender looked like.

If McMenemy was beginning to take over the tactical side of things from the ageing and increasingly out-of-touch and set-in-his-ways Maley, then Celtic also needed inspiring leadership on the field. This came from Lyon who, like Stein and McNeill in later years, was quite clearly a leader, and was made captain from an early stage.

The effect was electric and immediate. The Scottish League was won in 1936 after a decade of disappointment, the Scottish Cup the following year as crowds returned in huge numbers and then in 1938 a glorious treble of the Scottish League, the Glasgow Charity Cup and the all-British Empire Exhibition Trophy, making Celtic the best team in Great Britain and causing the half-back line of Geatons, Lyon and Paterson to roll off the tongue in the same way as Young, Loney and Hay had done a generation earlier.

It was not just the cool, inspirational and reassuring presence of Willie Lyon that mattered – it was also his ability to read a game, to encourage the hugely talented MacDonald and Delaney, to supply the ever-eager McGrory and Crum, and to perfect a 'special relationship' between himself and goalkeeper Joe Kennaway which was neither Scottish nor Irish, but English and Canadian!

Hitler saw to it that this great team did not last. Indeed it had waned by 1939, but Lyon deserves great credit for his leadership of one of the best teams in Celtic's history. We are hardly surprised to learn that his bravery and leadership manifested themselves in a different form a few years later, for Major William Lyon won the Military Cross in North Africa in 1943. After the war, he was assistant manager with Dundee, but did not find that job to his liking and returned to England and a life outside of football. He was only 50 when he died in 1962.

IRISH FLAG

An Irish flag has always flown at Celtic Park in honour of the nationality of the club's founders. From time to time bigots have tut-tutted at this sort of thing, and never more so than in 1952 when in the wake of some hooliganism at the New Year fixture, the SFA tried to persuade Celtic to remove the flag. Celtic, under chairman Sir Bob Kelly did not so much refuse to comply with the order as quietly and calmly, and with great dignity, ignore it. The SFA were supported in their absurd stance by, of all people, Hibs (yes, Hibs whose very name means 'people of Ireland'!) but Celtic enjoyed the support of Rangers (old friends always stick together and not without cause do we speak about the Old Firm!) and eventually the general public opinion of Scotland who began to rather enjoy the spectacle of the SFA making a fool of itself in insisting on something that they could not enforce! The flag remains to this day.

TOM 'TINY' WHARTON

He was called 'Tiny' because he was anything but – Wharton was a huge figure of a man, matching Jock Stein in bulk, and he was the foremost referee of the 1960s. He had many encounters with Celtic. On New Year's Day 1965, it was his duty to send off Jimmy Johnstone who had had a spat with Theorolf Beck of Rangers, a man who recovered astonishingly well. Tiny said, 'Well, Jimmy, I'm afraid you have to go for that one. What's your name?' Jimmy, about half the size of Tiny, said 'Roy Rogers' (a well known cowboy singer of the 1950s). 'All right, Roy, away you go and join Trigger in the stable!' (Trigger was Roy Rogers' horse).

On another occasion, Tiny (incredibly) was refused admission to Parkhead for a game he was meant to be officiating in because he had forgotten his pass. Tiny said to the jobsworth who clearly did not recognise him, 'Tell, Mr Stein that, if he wonders why there is no game today because the referee has not turned up, I will be waiting in the car park to discuss the matter with him.' It was one of the few times that Jock Stein was ever known to apologise to a referee.

ANDY WITH THE BILLIARD TABLE LEGS

Andy McAtee came from Croy, a younger contemporary of Jimmy Quinn. He was a fast right winger with a devastating shot from the legs that were said to resemble those of a billiard table. He joined the club in 1910, and very soon made his debut, impressing all who saw him with his speed and ability to score goals from tight angles. By the end of 1910/11, a disappointing season for Celtic in which they lost their league title but nevertheless managed to win the Scottish Cup, Andy won a Scottish Cup medal, being introduced into the replayed final against Hamilton Accies, and thus being part of the three Crojans (men from Croy) in that team alongside the mighty Quinn and his near namesake Tommy McAteer. Very soon after that he teamed-up with Patsy Gallacher to become the most devastating right wing partnership in the business, their finest hour being the Scottish League and Cup double of 1914.

Being a miner meant that he was in a reserved occupation for most of the war and was thus able to play for Celtic from 1914 to 1917, but he was conscripted at the end of the war and saw service in the forgotten theatre of the Italian Alps. He returned in January 1919 to play a great part in the league championship victories of 1919 and 1922.

But for the war, he might have won more Scottish caps than his solitary one at Wrexham in 1913, but he appeared many times for the Scottish League. After he left Celtic in 1924, he played in the United States. He died in 1956 and is buried not far from Jimmy Quinn in Kilsyth Cemetery.

> The Kaiser, they say
> Watched Andy one day
> And remarked, it is said
> 'Dearie me!'
> My German artillery's
> Just fit for the pillory
> They can't shoot like young McAtee!

THE GREEN BRIGADE

A phenomenon of recent years, the Green Brigade often provide some welcome atmosphere on dull days. At Celtic Park they sit (or stand) in the north-east corner of the ground singing songs which are not always approved of, but their support is real and total and is surely to be encouraged.

THE SHAMROCK

This was the first-ever Celtic fanzine and was produced in the bad old days of 1963 and 1964 from an Edinburgh base, edited by a man called Dougan from Gilmerton Dykes and sold on match days by a man with a shabby coat and down-at-the-heel shoes ('long down-trodden man', he was called). The paper was poor and the typing amateurish, but it was very much the voice of the people at a time when their voice needed to be heard. It did not hold back from criticism of the players and management when necessary. Among other things, it said that Bobby Murdoch, at that time an inferior inside forward would be a better right-half, and this was long before Stein came and implemented that. It seemed to disappear just about the time in 1965 when the corner was turned, and it is to be hoped that the 'long down-trodden man' lived long enough to enjoy Lisbon.

HEARTS FANS INVADE
THE JUNGLE

It is Glasgow in January and it is raining heavily. There is no shelter on the 'away' terracing – or 'Rangers end' – so what can a poor Hearts fan do? All he can do is come into the Jungle where there is some sort of cover, inadequate though it is with the holes in the roof. Normally there would be no room, for it would be packed with Celtic fans and no Hearts fan would have the courage, but this is 16 January 1965 when Celtic are on their knees and in the crowd of about 20,000 Celtic fans are almost outnumbered by

Hearts fans, for their team is seemingly going for the league championship. Hearts win 3–1, and there now seems to be no hope for Celtic . . . unless of course they were to ask Jock Stein to be their manager!

DANNY OF THE MANY INJURIES

Danny McGrain, Celtic's best ever right-back, came through three horrendous crises in his professional life, any one of which would have floored a lesser man. On 25 March 1972 just as he was making his way into the Celtic team, he sustained a fractured skull in an awful clash of heads at Falkirk. He overcame that, but then during the 1974 World Cup in West Germany, perpetual raging thirst made him suspect that something was wrong and he was duly diagnosed as a diabetic. Once again, Danny coped with this, but at the start of the 1977/78 season a mysterious foot injury appeared – and it was this injury, as well as the transfer of Dalglish to Liverpool, which consigned Celtic to a barren and trophyless season and led to the departure of Jock Stein from the managerial chair. It was also a severe loss to Scotland, for had Danny gone to Argentina, things would surely never have been so bad. His playing ability would have made a difference, but so too would his level-headedness, a quality that surely would have taken the sting out of the trouble that the malcontents caused to the beleaguered Ally McLeod. Danny was no softie, nor was he a moaner and his perpetual popularity is deserved.

A HAT-TRICK OF PENALTIES

Bobby Collins achieved this remarkable (although by no means unique) feat on 26 September 1953 when in a 3–0 defeat of Aberdeen at Celtic Park in front of 26,000 fans, he scored three penalties.

AND THEY GAVE US JIMMY McGRORY

Even now, some 30 years after he died and some 75 years after he gave up playing, there will not be many alive who have not heard of James McGrory and who do not associate the name irreconcilably with Celtic. If they were ignorant of this mighty man, then all they have to do is listen to the first words of the Willie Maley song 'And they gave us James McGrory and . . .'

It was somehow fitting that McGrory was born some ten days after his predecessor and forerunner Jimmy Quinn scored his iconic hat-trick in the 1904 Scottish Cup final. He died in 1982 after a lifetime of service to the club, and is buried like so many old Celts in Dalbeth Cemetery, not far from Celtic Park.

It was a frosty, foggy midwinter's day in 1935 that he overtook the world goalscoring record in a game against Aberdeen at Celtic Park – the goal which actually broke the record was a remarkable one. A hard, low cross from Johnny Crum and McGrory, disdaining personal safety on the hard ground, dived full-length to bullet the ball into the roof of the net.

Young Celtic fans said to their dads
As midwinter fog hung hoary
You can keep your Santa Claus
'Cos I've got James McGrory.

He ended up with 440 league goals and 550 in all games.

THE CELTIC SONG

Released in October 1961 and sung by the Celtic-supporting Glen Daly, this song is still played at Celtic Park on match day. Some of the lyrics, such as 'we don't care if they win, lose or draw' (Oh, no?) and 'darn the hair we care', were crass, but were soon replaced by better and more obvious words, and this song has stood the test of time and remains a very rousing experience at a full Parkhead.

It was first heard being sung by supporters at a game on 4 November 1961 at a frosty Dens Park on the occasion of a 2–1 defeat. It was sung plaintively and with an as-yet imperfect command of the lyrics and melody by a group of young men at the back of the long obtuse-angled stand at Dens Park which is still in existence.

Its popularity grew rapidly as Celtic's young side hit a purple patch towards the end of 1961 with a 7–1 hammering of St Mirren, a 5–1 victory against Partick Thistle and a thrilling 4–3 win over Hibs. The song grew in popularity apace with the team's good performances and by the time that the team came to Kirkcaldy on 23 December, it was as if everyone was getting this record for Christmas, for the trains pulled into Kirkcaldy station and everyone seemed to get off singing 'Sure it's a grand old team to play for . . . and the Glasgow Celtic will be there.' Celtic won 4–0, Rangers lost that day and the team were on the crest of the wave. It was indeed Christmas.

The glory days seemed to have arrived but bad weather came after the festive period, knocking out the Motherwell and the Rangers games. Things might have been different that 1961/62 season if the team had been allowed to keep going, but there was no stopping 'The Celtic Song'. It was sung loudly and universally by the time we beat Hearts in a thrilling cup tie in mid-February and then an even better game against Third Lanark when the team, inspired by the song, fought back to get a 4–4 draw, compelling the replay to be moved from Cathkin to Hampden because of the huge crowd expected. The precaution was justified, for over 51,000 turned up on a Wednesday night to sing the song at full volume as Celtic, after an uncertain first half, hit top gear and beat Thirds 4–0.

Yes they were heady days – and the song played a part – but then came St Mirren at Ibrox and a woeful display.

The song on the other side – 'An Irishman's Dream' – was good as well and was sung as if by an Irish American about the Shannon flowing down Broadway, etc. – the American equivalent of 'If we only had old Ireland over here' which was of course set in Australia.

'The Celtic Song' continued to develop – perhaps Lisbon in 1967 was 'the show' referred to? After all, Bertie Auld started singing it in the tunnel, did he not? The Italians must have wondered what or who they were up against.

One day at Tannadice Park when the Celtic choir were at full volume achieving their crescendo with, 'and the GLASGOW CELTIC WILL BE THERE!', a brave young girl with a Dundee United scarf (in the early 1960s fans stood together without any segregation) then delivered two immortal add-on words – 'Selling Programmes!'

AMAZING BUT TRUE

Surely no-one in world football has made his debut in more bizarre circumstances than Willie Goldie. Willie was one of the reserve team goalkeepers but, on 1 October 1960, wasn't playing for anyone, so he decided to go along to see the first team playing at Airdrie. So there he was standing waiting at a bus stop, green and white scarf tied round his neck, for the normal service bus to take him to Airdrie. Suddenly a bus stopped for him, but it wasn't the service bus, it was the Celtic team bus. Chairman Bob Kelly had seen him standing there and ordered the driver to stop and give him a lift. Slightly embarrassed Willie got on, greeted with cries of 'Who's this hooligan?' and 'No bottle throwing to-day, Willie!' It got worse, for suddenly Bob Kelly decided that Willie was playing and poor John Fallon, the regular goalkeeper, was informed that he would be watching the game from the stand. Had this ploy succeeded, Bob Kelly would have been looked upon as a genius. As it was, Airdrie won 2–0 and poor Willie had a bad game and never played for Celtic again!

HE STARTED IT ALL!

In a side which has been famous for goalscorers, Sandy 'The Duke' McMahon was the first to excite the support. Yet he was an unlikely character for several reasons. One was that he was from the east of Scotland (Selkirk probably, although there is another Alexander McMahon born in Dundee) and the other was that he did not look like a centre forward, lacking the broad shoulders of Jimmy Quinn and Jimmy McGrory in subsequent years. He looked awkward and ungainly, but had a tremendous ability to swerve and deceive a defence.

He was prevailed upon to go to Nottingham Forest in 1892 to play professional football. Scottish football was still amateur, but somehow or other Celtic were able to persuade him to return and it is hard to believe that there was not some kind of 'payment' offered. He played in Celtic's first three Scottish Cup finals – 1892, 1899 and 1900 – and scored in all of them. Arguably his best single performance was the Glasgow Charity Cup final of May 1895 when he scored a hat-trick against Rangers, the final goal being a header 'with a Ranger hanging from each leg' according to a particularly graphic account. Willie Maley described McMahon as the 'best header of a ball I have ever seen,' and that from a man who managed Quinn and McGrory! He could play at centre forward or inside left in which position he struck up a telepathic understanding with Johnny Campbell and created a devastating left-wing duo. He played his part in the winning of the league in 1893, 1894, 1896 and 1898.

The Duke was chosen to play for Scotland six times but only once against England – at Celtic Park in 1894 when he scored Scotland's goal in the 1–1 draw – and it was felt he deserved more international honours than he got. His one real bad day for Celtic came on New Year's Day 1902 when he was sent off for losing his temper at the referee, Mr Nisbet of Cowdenbeath. The score was 1–1 at the time (McMahon himself having scored) but Rangers went on to win the game and the championship.

He played for Partick Thistle for a season before he retired to become a publican. A man of literary inclination with a tremendous knowledge of Burns and Shakespeare, Sandy died while still a young man in 1916 and is buried besides loads of other blessed Celts in Dalbeth Cemetery.

NOT CHOSEN AGAINST CELTIC ONE DAY BUT PLAYING FOR THEM THE NEXT

John Atkinson was a young amateur, a medical student, playing for Hamilton Academical in April 1909. He would have been disappointed not to have been picked to play against Celtic at Parkhead on 21 Wednesday April, for opportunities to play against this mighty team did not come every day. He sat in the pavilion and watched a 1–1 draw. Celtic's left winger, Davie Hamilton, known as 'the Dancer' was injured in this game and unavailable for the next day's game against Morton. With no recognised left winger available on their books, Maley approached Hamilton Accies before they left Parkhead that day and asked, in a joke, if they had a left winger handy. The answer was that yes, they had John Atkinson. As he was an amateur, there was no problem about registration and John duly was asked to play. The young student must have thought he was being 'had' – not chosen to play for his own team against the mighty Celts one day, he was now playing for them the next! His daydream continued the next day, for he scored the first and fourth goals in Celtic's 5–1 win over Morton and had his hand shaken by the great Jimmy Quinn for doing so! In the last game of the season, Celtic played at Douglas Park, Hamilton. Once again, John Atkinson was not considered good enough to get a game for Hamilton and had to sit in the stand watching Celtic beat the Accies to win the league. One would imagine that he rather enjoyed that! In later years as a practising GP in the north of England, he could tell his incredulous patients that he played for Celtic and helped them win their fifth Scottish League title in a row in 1909.

NAPOLEON

One of the greatest inside forwards that Scottish football has ever seen, Jimmy McMenemy was nicknamed 'Napoleon', and played for Celtic between 1902 and 1920, followed by Partick Thistle until 1922, and then, briefly, Stenhousemuir. He also won twelve caps for Scotland and holds the record for being Scotland's third oldest player (only Davie Weir and Jim Leighton beat him) when he played for Scotland against Ireland at Celtic Park in March 1920 at the age of 39 years 203 days.

He signed from Rutherglen Glencairn in May 1902 and scored in his debut against Port Glasgow in November of that year. He was one of the mainstays of the great Celtic side of the Edwardian era, where the 'inside triangle' of Young at right-half, Bennett on the right wing and Napoleon at inside right was 'a sight to behold' on many occasions, and of the other great Celtic side immediately before and during the First World War. He had made his reputation at inside right, but agreed to move to inside left to allow his prodigiously talented protégé Patsy Gallacher to take his place on the right side. Napoleon was equally at home in either position and scored a remarkable number of goals from the inside positions – notably a mazy dribble and shot in the New Year's Day hammering of Rangers at Parkhead in 1914, but his strength lay in his accurate passing, and his knowledge of the game which led Maley to say that, to Napoleon, the football pitch was like a chess board.

His record of eleven Scottish League medals and seven Scottish Cup medals (one with Partick Thistle in 1921) speaks for itself. His international career is distinguished by the part he played in Scotland's victories against England in 1910 and

1914. Illness and war service seemed to have put an end to his career in 1918, but he returned to play a glorious part in the league championship victory of 1919. The decision to 'pay him off' in 1920 at the age of 40 was not without its critics, but Napoleon went to Partick Thistle where he won a Scottish Cup medal with them in 1921 in a 1–0 victory over Rangers in April 1921.

Having twice coached for Partick Thistle, Napoleon was brought back to be the trainer for Celtic in October 1934. Given the advancing years and infirmity of manager Willie Maley, this in fact meant that he ran the team, and he therefore deserves great credit for the fine Celtic side of that era, which distinguished itself by winning the Scottish League in 1936 and 1938, the Scottish Cup in 1937 and the Empire Exhibition Trophy of 1938. Had he been appointed Maley's successor in 1940, Celtic's war record would have been substantially different. His son John McMenemy played for Celtic and Motherwell, his other son Harry played for Newcastle United and the legendary Southampton manager Lawrie McMenemy is his great-nephew.

> Oh dear what can the matter be?
> Rangers got beat by Celtic on Saturday
> Two goals from Quinn and one from McMenemy
> Oh what fun it was there!

RAFAEL SCHEIDT

There was no easy way of pronouncing this fellow's name. It did indeed sound like the vulgar word for excrement. He joined the club in the 1999/2000 season but mercifully, his stay was brief. Cruel people said his play reflected his name.

ECK THE ICICLE

Sometimes it is difficult to express in mere words the contribution of a man to the Celtic cause. From Stenhousemuir, Alec McNair joined the club in 1903 and was a mainstay of the great Celtic side that won six league championships in a row between 1905 and 1910, then another four between 1914 and 1917, and yet another two in 1919 and 1922 before his eventual retirement in 1925. His 584 league appearances for the Parkhead side actually tops those of Billy McNeill, but Billy McNeill played more games if all competitions are counted.

'Eck' was mainly a right-back, but was such a versatile defender that in 1907 when Celtic became the first team to win the Scottish League and Cup double he played mainly at centre-half as Willie Loney was out with a broken arm for most of the season. He won the Scottish Cup six times between 1907 and 1923, as well as fifteen caps for Scotland, a number that would have been greatly increased if it had not been for the First World War. His best game for Scotland was in April 1914, when the team beat England 3–1 and 'McNair never gave Smith or Mosscrop a kick of the ball'. Eck was the right-back of the two famous Celtic teams that began 'Adams, McNair and Orr' and 'Shaw, McNair and Dodds'. He tended to be the more defensive-minded of the two full-backs, allowing left-back Joe Dodds or centre-half Willie Loney to become the sixth forward on occasion. Intelligent, thoughtful and gentlemanly, he was so cool under pressure that he was called 'the Icicle', and it is a matter of some surprise that he was never made captain of Celtic until after the First World War, when he was captain of Scotland for a short while as well. In that he was a tremendous success as a diplomat and a fine example of what Scotland should be.

His personal life was tragic, for his wife died in 1915 and he had to bring up a family on his own, but he wasn't called 'the Icicle' for nothing and addressed his own problems in the same way that he defended for Celtic – methodically, calmly and conscientiously. As late as 1923 when he was near his 40th birthday, McNair won his last Scottish Cup medal in the 1–0 win against Hibs, calming everyone down in Hibs' late onslaught.

When his lengthy career came to a halt in 1925, he became manager of Dundee for a while, but met with little success. In his later years he was also a referee supervisor, but his career outside football was in stockbroking. Celtic and Maley owed a great deal to Eck McNair.

HAPPY BIRTHDAY, MR MALEY!

Willie Maley was born on 25 April 1868 at Newry. On three occasions, he celebrated his birthday with a league championship.

25 April 1908 saw Celtic beat Rangers 1–0 at Ibrox, a week after they had won the Scottish Cup. It was a rough game at Ibrox with both Jimmy Quinn and Jimmy McMenemy injured by brutal tackles, but Alec Bennett scored the only goal of the game, and Maley thus reached his 40th birthday at the peak of his career, having managed his team to back-to-back Scottish League and Cup doubles.

25 April 1910 saw Celtic clinch their sixth league championship in a 0–0 draw against Hibs at Celtic Park before a paltry crowd of 2,000. It was a Monday afternoon after Celtic had lost 2–0 to Falkirk at Brockville on the Saturday. This game had thus an air of anti-climax about it, but no doubt Maley celebrated his 42nd birthday in style.

25 April 1936 saw Celtic, even without the injured McGrory, beat Partick Thistle 3–1 at Firhill to put an end to a wretched ten years of under-achievement and win the league championship for the first time since 1926. Maley was now 68, and he showed few signs of wishing to retire.

RECORD ATTENDANCES

Celtic and record attendances go together, for they hold the record attendance for the Scottish League, Scottish Cup, Scottish League Cup and European Cup.

Scottish League	Rangers v Celtic	Ibrox	2 January 1939	118,567
Scottish Cup	Celtic v Aberdeen	Hampden	24 April 1937	147,365
Scottish League Cup	Celtic v Rangers	Hampden	23 October 1965	107,609
European Cup	Celtic v Leeds United	Hampden	15 April 1970	135,826

Attendances for the Glasgow Cup and Glasgow Charity Cup are harder to pin down, but it is a fair bet that Celtic would feature in the record attendances for both competitions.

A week before the Scottish Cup final of 1937 (mentioned on the previous page), Hampden saw an even bigger crowd of 149,547 for the Scotland v England game and one player played in both games – Jimmy Delaney! And he was on the winning side both times!

THE McSTAY DYNASTY

A total of four McStays have played for Celtic, two brothers in the 1920s who were great-uncles of the two brothers who played in the 1980s. On four occasions – 1923, 1925, 1927 and 1985 two brothers McStay won Scottish Cup medals. Willie and Jimmy played in the 1920s and Willie and Paul played in the 1980s. Jimmy, of course, was the manager during the war years, and Willie junior had a career in management as well, although not for Celtic.

Willie Senior

Sometimes called 'the tank' (he had served in the First World War) because of his rugged defending, Willie McStay senior (sometimes written McStey in newspaper reports and certainly pronounced by the fans as if it rhymed with the vowel in 'mighty' hence the frequent headlines of 'mighty McStey') was at home anywhere in the defence although he always said that left-back was his favourite position. He was also an inspirational captain, a brilliant tactician and a reliable taker of penalty kicks. He made his debut on the opening day of the 1916/17 season and held his place in that very fine side which lost only on the penultimate league game and conceded only 19 goals all season –

something that did a great deal to cheer supporters up in the face of grim news elsewhere. He then took part in the latter stages of the war, but came back to dominate Celtic's defence throughout the decade of the 1920s. While other players like Gilchrist, Cassidy, Cringan and McInally threw tantrums and caused trouble, McStay remained like a rock to rally players and supporters. He was not immune to disaffection, however, nor the 'insidious effects of socialism', and history has not been kind to him in terms of why he was not in the team that lost the Glasgow Charity Cup semi-final against Rangers in 1923 (he was apparently in the USA considering a career there).

An intelligent and well-read, gentle, urbane man, Willie realised in 1925 that Rangers were a better team, but before the famous semi-final, concocted with Patsy Gallacher the plan that defeated them 5–0, withdrawing totally into defence for the first half of the game and then hitting them hard in the second. He had the ability to nurture young vulnerable players like Connolly, Thomson and McGrory, and it is difficult to overstate Willie's contribution to the cause throughout the difficult decade of the 1920s.

He played equally well for Scotland, latterly as captain, and was in the side that beat England 2–0 at Hampden in 1925 when Scotland won the treble, and was captain a year later when they won 1–0 at Manchester. In 1927, however, he made the tactless remark about how Scotland's defeat was all due to his full-back partner Bob Thomson of Falkirk – something that Falkirk people never forgave him for.

He was 35 when he left Celtic in 1929 after over a decade of consistent service. He subsequently had a short time with Hearts then dabbled in Irish football before retiring to his Lanarkshire home and his passion for dogs.

Jimmy

History tends to confuse Jimmy with his elder brother Willie. They were both defenders, frequently played in the same team, winning Scottish Cup medals together three times in the 1920s, but whereas it was generally agreed that Willie was the better player (he was capped for Scotland 13 times whereas Jimmy's only International honours were for the Scottish League), Jimmy was possibly the better captain.

He took over from Willie as captain in 1929, and it was his fortune to lead the team in the tempestuous year of 1931 with the epic Scottish Cup final win over Motherwell, the ground-breaking tour of North America and the tragic events of the death of John Thomson. McStay earned great respect and admiration from everyone for the dignified way in which he led the club during the traumatic aftermath of that event. Further tragedy would of course visit the club when Peter Scarff took ill and eventually died of tuberculosis.

A trifle slow on the ground, he was imperious in the air and had tremendous passing ability. He was an attack-minded centre-half in the tradition of Willie Loney whom he admired so much, and possibly Celtic lost rather too many goals because of his commitment to this role, but his greatest contribution to the club was in his inspirational leadership, so often being the voice of Maley on the field, and being able to bring out the best in key players like Peter Wilson, Alec Thomson and of course the goalscoring machine Jimmy McGrory.

He won five Scottish Cup medals in all, but only one Scottish League medal (in 1926 before he became captain). He was disappointed in this, but he never gave less than his best for his beloved Celtic. He went on to play for Hamilton Accies in 1934, and after managing Alloa immediately before the Second World War, became Maley's successor in January

1940. In this, he was no great success, but the times were by no means easy in wartime and the Celtic board seemed to lack any great commitment to gaining the success that would have meant so much to their support.

Paul

Paul McStay was generally recognised as being one of the best players of his day. A succession of Scotland team managers certainly thought that, for he was capped 76 times, and his paltry collection of medals (disproportionately low in comparison with his playing ability) can be explained by the undeniable fact that he came at a bad time of internal political strife and team managers who were visibly not of the Maley or Stein mould.

The best of these managers, Billy McNeill, gave him his chance in early 1982. Paul was a creative midfield player with great passing ability, an eye for goal and a clear desire to do well for the club that he loved and never left, however hard the media tried to persuade him to go. He had first come to the world's attention for the Scottish Schoolboys when they beat their English counterparts at Wembley in 1980, and, unlike a few of his contemporaries, Paul did live up to his promise, looking particularly good in 1982 when he very soon established himself as one of the best players in the country. But the Nicholas fiasco of 1983 and the departure of McNeill soon after gave McStay his first taste of the problems that would beset Celtic for most of his career, namely political instability, power seeking and the club in the hands of people who knew little about football and even less about what the club meant to so many people.

Paul's best season was of course the centenary season of 1987/88 when he played his full part in the glories that unfolded, but that was short-lived and after many heartbreaks, especially after he became captain in 1990, he may have thought of leaving the club. In 1992, on one famous occasion at the end of the season, he threw his shirt into the Jungle.

But he didn't go. Although he was one of the more stable and reliable figures in the chaos of 1993 and 1994, his form was never the same again, even after things stabilised under McCann. He had the misfortune to miss a penalty in the awful League Cup final shoot-out of 1994, but captained the side to the Scottish Cup in 1995 in a poor game against Airdrie.

Paul's problem was that he was not naturally aggressive nor a glory-hunter. Possibly he lacked some of the 'devil' that other players of commensurate ability, like Jim Baxter or Denis Law had, but he still brought to the game some fine play. Even in the days when Celtic played badly, supporters could rely on at least a flash of genius from Paul McStay. He limped off the field at Stark's Park, Kirkcaldy, in April 1997 and disappeared out of the game altogether. He now lives in Sydney, Australia.

Willie Junior

Willie McStay junior was a good full-back who won a Scottish Cup medal in 1985 and a league medal in 1986. He managed a few teams like Sligo Rovers and Ross County and was a coach at Celtic Park.

IBROX

Oddly enough, Ibrox has not always been an unlucky ground for Celtic. The Empire Exhibiton Trophy was won there in

1938, the Scottish Cup in 1892, 1900, 1911, 1912, 1914 and the Scottish League Cup in 1997/98. There is also the surprising fact that in the two seasons that Celtic won every trophy they entered – 1908 and 1967 – they secured the league championship at Ibrox.

NEIL MOCHAN

Neil Mochan made a remarkable and telling contribution to the fortunes of Celtic FC over a period of more than 30 years as a player and trainer. He was known as 'Smiler' or the 'Cannonball Kid' and was immensely popular with the fans, although a little less so with the Celtic establishment who tended to drop him from time to time, whimsically and for no apparent reason, particularly during the 1954/55 season when Mochan might well have made the difference between success and failure in Celtic's attempt to win the double for the second successive season.

He could play virtually anywhere in the forward line, although his best position was left winger. For a stocky individual he was surprisingly fast, and he had a magnificent left foot which brought many goals for the club, hence the 'cannonball' nickname. He was not well liked by chairman Bob Kelly, apparently because he was once fined in court for the mildly outrageous 'crime' of not possessing a licence for his radio!

He had begun his career with Morton, but joined Celtic from Middlesbrough in spring 1953 and then went on to win a couple of medals for the club before he had even played a game at Celtic Park. These were the Glasgow Charity Cup and the Coronation Cup – and he scored in both finals!

Success then followed in the shape of a league and cup double in 1954 and Scotland recognition, but he cannot have enjoyed the 1954 World Cup finals in Switzerland which included a 7–0 defeat by Uruguay in which Mochan would recall that the advice given to the team consisted of little more than 'get stuck in!'

He played in the side that won Celtic's first ever Scottish League Cup in October 1956, but was immortalised by the League Cup final of the following year in which he scored twice in the 7–1 beating of Rangers. He flirted with a defensive role for a spell before returning to the forward line and on one famous occasion, scored all five goals that Celtic put past St Mirren in a replayed cup tie in February 1960.

Later that year, he was off on his travels to Dundee United and later Raith Rovers, but on giving up the playing side, he was appointed trainer at Celtic Park in 1964. His influence was already strong, but when Stein came a year later, Mochan was the man who made the young Celtic team the fittest and fastest in football. He stayed as trainer/coach until 1991 when he was appointed kit manager. He died of leukaemia in Falkirk in 1994.

WALK OUT

It was the dreadful night of 15 May 1963 when 50,000 almost of one accord literally turned their backs on Celtic (not to do the huddle as they do in more modern and happier times) and walked out of Hampden. This was to express their disgust at what they were seeing after Rangers scored their third goal in the Scottish Cup replay. It was an eerie, surreal experience and anyone who said that in four years time Celtic would be the first team to bring the European Cup back to Britain would have been deemed a candidate for a visit to a psychiatrist.

BOBBY MURDOCH – DIFFERENT CLASS

If one was ever asked to name the best player of the Lisbon Lions team, it would be difficult not to come up with the name of Bobby Murdoch. Certainly his opponents from Helenio Herrera downwards thought so, for he was the powerhouse of the team from whom everything flowed. His relentless energy, visionary passing ability, sheer power and ball-winning earned him the adjective 'world class'.

He made his debut at the start of the 1962/63 season, scoring the first goal against Hearts at Parkhead, but this was an unfortunate season to make a debut, for the team was not without talent but they suffered an incredibly bad run with the forward line in particular which was chopped and changed capriciously by inadequate management. Disaster struck the club with a Scottish Cup final replay defeat to Rangers after Murdoch had scored an equaliser in the first game.

Discerning supporters saw that he would be a better midfield man than a forward, and it was Jock Stein who made this change in 1965, after which the team simply took off to reach dizzy and scarcely believable heights of Scottish and European domination with Murdoch the mainstay of a team which was not short of stars. Trophies which had eluded Murdoch and Celtic before 1965 suddenly became regular visitors to Celtic Park. Bobby was never at his best when playing for Scotland, and this was a shame for Murdoch at his best might even have won a World Cup for Scotland. As it was he was favourably compared with the great Celtic right-halves of history – and there has been no shortage of them, like Peter Wilson, Bobby Evans and Jimmy Young – and no less a man than Jimmy McGrory thought he was the best of them all.

Yet Murdoch had his problems. He very nearly missed Lisbon with an ankle problem (a problem which would stay with him all his life) and he had a recurring problem with his weight, causing Jock Stein on two occasions to send him to a health farm for special treatment. Stein would not have done this for a lesser man.

In 1973 he moved on to Middlesbrough. Some thought that Stein moved him on when he still had something to offer Celtic, but in the north-east of England, he became a hero for the sadly underperforming Teesside outfit, working well with Jack Charlton and playing an influential part in the development of the young Graeme Souness before himself becoming their coach and manager. He was sacked by Boro in 1982 and returned to Glasgow. Sadly health problems plagued him all the rest of his life, but he remained the humble and lovable Bobby Murdoch. When one met him, one would never have thought that he was one of the greatest players ever to grace the earth.

SCAPULARS

What are scapulars? They are mini-shoulder pads often worn by members of a religious order. In the case of Willie Kivlichan, he was a member of the Third Order of St Francis and scapulars were required even when playing football. On

1 October 1910, Kivlichan was playing for Celtic against Queen's Park at Hampden and his scapulars escaped from beneath his green and white jersey and were clearly seen by the crowd. According to the devoutly Catholic *Glasgow Observer* this sight 'brought tears of joy to the eyes of the Parkhead faithful' – a touch of exaggeration here, one feels, and as Kivlichan previously played for Rangers, one wonders what the reaction might have been there.

WILL YOU NO COME BACK AGAIN?

Ibrox on 26 March 1927 witnessed an amazing sight at the Scottish Cup semi-final between Celtic and Falkirk. It is not uncommon for ex-Celts to be heartily booed by the fans that used to loved them. Dalglish and Nicholas, for example, were left in no doubt that 'furthering their career' cut little ice with the Celtic faithful, but in 1927 Falkirk had Patsy Gallacher, generally believed to be the greatest player of his era and by some to be the greatest Celt of all time. It was felt that Celtic had allowed him to leave too early, and when, before this game, an attempt was made at community singing by the conductor of the Govan Instrumental Band, the selections included the Jacobite anthem 'Will you no' come back again?' The words could hardly have been more appropriate to Celtic supporters' feelings about Patsy, and the song was sung with gusto and indeed continued all game with Patsy cheered to the echo every time he touched the ball. He played brilliantly, enjoying the bizarre appreciation of the opposition support, but Celtic won 1–0 thanks to an Adam McLean goal.

THE BOY FROM CROY

No-one dominated conversation in Edwardian Scotland more than Jimmy Quinn, the man who in so many ways typified the Celtic team of that era with his legendary goalscoring. He was a very shy man, however, with no great desire to be anything other than Jimmy Quinn of Celtic.

His first few years with the club were not happy ones – he had been involved, for example, in the Scottish Cup final defeats of 1901 and 1902, and more than once, he expressed a desire to return to the mines of Croy, but Maley persuaded him otherwise. For a long time no-one seemed able to decide whether his best position was on the left wing or in the centre, but it was as centre forward that he scored his two famous hat-tricks against Rangers, one in the Coronation Cup of 1902 and the other more famous one in the Scottish Cup final of 1904 after Celtic had been two down.

He was no shrinking violet on the field and twice, in 1905 and 1907, earned lengthy suspensions for being ordered off in games against Rangers. In both cases there was an element of injustice, but Jimmy fought back and answered all his critics by performances on the field, scoring legendary goals like the one against Kilmarnock on Christmas Day 1909, or the Glasgow Cup final of 1909 when four Rangers players knocked him to the ground, but he still managed to score!

Many of his goals were scored through the now illegal 'shoulder-charging' of opponents and goalkeepers in particular, and for this he was well equipped with his 'bison' shoulders, but he was also speedy, distributed the ball well, could head the ball and had a devastating shot, making full use of the excellent service of Somers, McMenemy and the 'Holy Trinity' of Young, Loney and Hay.

He was capped eleven times for Scotland, his most famous appearances being in Dublin in 1908 when he scored four goals and then in 1910 when he masterminded Scotland to their 2–0 win over England at Hampden earning the accolade with the English press as being 'the best in Britain'. Music hall audiences in Glasgow and Edinburgh now sang 'Jimmy Quinn' instead of 'Clementine' as their darling!

Increasingly injury-prone in later years, Jimmy played his last game for Celtic in 1915 before retiring to work in the mines in his native Croy, the village that he has immortalised, emerging every Saturday to watch his beloved Celtic until his death in 1945. He would be frequently seen with his clay pipe and amazed everyone by 'looking just like an ordinary man'.

FLOODS OF TEARS?

Willo Flood played for Celtic for a brief time between 2009 and 2010. What makes him remarkable, however, are the events on the eve of his arrival on 29 January 2009. It was two days before the closing of the transfer window and Celtic were playing Dundee United in the Scottish League Cup semi-final. It was an open secret that Willo Flood was on the verge of being transferred to Celtic, but that night at Hampden he was still playing for Dundee United (on loan from Cardiff City).

It was a close game as 90 minutes came and went with no goals scored. Extra time was similar although Celtic hit the woodwork on more than one occasion, and it came down to penalties. Willo took the first one for United and just as all the conspiracy theorists were planning their arguments for tomorrow, Willo scored. So that was that, then, wasn't it? No. The teams still could not be separated. Both teams missed one each, but everyone else (goalkeepers Artur Boruc and Łukasz Załuska included) scored and we had to start again! So Willo took another penalty . . . and this time he hit the bar and the ball went over. Scott McDonald then sunk a penalty and Celtic reached the final.

So was it all deliberate then on the part of Willo? Well no, actually, because he had deprived himself of the chance of a medal because he couldn't play for Celtic in the final anyway, as he was cup-tied for Dundee United! Willo was just simply an unlucky player who missed a penalty.

TEN INTERNATIONALS AND . . .

Charlie Shaw was a legend in a team which is already rich in goalkeepers – Dan McArthur, Davie Adams, John Thomson, Ronnie Simpson and many others – and yet the paradox is that he was never capped for Scotland at a time when other members of the team were. Celtic were frequently referred to as 'ten Internationals and Charlie Shaw', but there are reasons for Charlie's lack of international recognition. In the first place, his best years coincided with the First World War when all Scotland games were suspended, but the other reason is that Scotland had plenty of other good goalkeepers around as well. In any case, by 1918 Charlie was 33 years old.

Charlie was an immensely popular figure at Celtic Park. From the Celtic heartland of Twechar, Charlie had played in English football before he came to Parkhead, and in his first home appearance for the club on 10 May 1913, he won a medal in the Charity Cup final against Rangers. From then on he was an integral part of the team which won four league championships in a row, and with McNair and Dodds, formed an almost impenetrable defence registering a clean sheet in 26 out of the 38 league games in the triumphant 1913/14 season.

He was lithe with great reflexes, but more than that, he radiated confidence, looking like everyone's favourite uncle, and, given the general excellence of the team, it was small wonder that stories circulated about him wandering round to ask the other goalkeeper if he needed a hand or going home for his tea when he got fed up. In the calendar year of 1916, Charlie conceded 18 goals in 42 games – and Celtic won every game! When Sunny Jim got injured in September 1916, it was Charlie who became the captain where his leadership skills and kindly advice came to the fore.

In the early 1920s the team began to struggle a little more, and Charlie was worked harder, but he never let the team down and there was no more loved character at Celtic Park than Charlie. Even the song that the Rangers supporters made up about him not seeing where 'Alan Morton pit the ba' (copied by every other team – Alec Troup of Dundee, Willie Hillhouse of Third Lanark and Tokey Duncan of Raith Rovers all did the same, apparently) was a great compliment to Charlie and accepted as such by him.

He was nearly forty when he eventually lost his place to Peter Shevlin, and in summer 1925 he sailed to America to play there. He met the Celtic party when they came there in 1931 and had a long chat with John Thomson on the art of goalkeeping. Tragically both these men would die within the next decade, but there was never a more popular character than Charlie Shaw.

BACKS TO THE WALL

13 April 1918 was the day that it all ended for Celtic, and it almost all ended for the British Empire as well. The German Ludendorff Offensive had been launched a month before and was clearly succeeding with a breakthrough to the Channel looking likely. Field Marshal Douglas Haig had issued his 'backs to the wall' order on the Thursday, and by the Saturday wild rumours were sweeping across Glasgow about a British surrender. But Celtic, league champions for the past four years, had the visit of the quickly improving Motherwell to deal with at Parkhead for their last league game of the season, while Rangers had the less-than-impressive Clyde at Ibrox. Both teams were level on points, and if both teams had won, there would probably have been a play-off as there had been in 1905.

Without being in any way too impressive, Rangers beat Clyde 2–1 but Celtic were held to a draw. Patsy Gallacher scored halfway through the second half, but then Motherwell took advantage of shoddy defending from the makeshift Celtic half-back line to equalise just on half time. The second half was one of constant Celtic attack as Patsy Gallacher ('the most talked about man in the trenches') and Jimmy 'Napoleon' McMenemy inspired Celtic – but they simply could not score as Motherwell's defence of Rundell, Robertson, McSkimming, McIntosh, Finlayson and Stewart held out 'with their backs to the wall' as a Sunday paper put it. Rangers thus won the league (they had invested a considerable amount of money to hire guest players all through the season), and 30,000 frustrated Celtic fans left Parkhead to face what seemed like an uncertain future. It wasn't all that bad, though, for before the end of the season, they won the

War Shield Fund trophy and the Glasgow Charity Cup – and of course, the British Army with considerable help from the French and (decisively) the Americans eventually held the line and turned the tide of the First World War.

THE THOMSON PILGRIMS

Most people know that 5 September 1931 was Celtic's saddest day when goalkeeper John Thomson was accidentally killed at Ibrox (he collided with an opposition player and suffered a fractured skull). Fewer are aware of the hundreds of Celtic supporters who walked from Glasgow to attend his funeral at Cardenden on Wednesday 9 September. They had little option because this was 1931 and the depth of the depression. Eighty years later in early September 2011 an intrepid group of about 50 supporters performed the walk to commemorate this occasion.

THE POWDER MONKEY

Peter Somers has been grossly undervalued by Celtic historians, although never by his team-mates nor his manager Willie Maley who was quite happy to describe him as 'the powder monkey'. The image was a good one, for a 'powder monkey' was usually a small man (so that he could even crawl inside a cannon to pack the ammunition in, if necessary) who would load the cannon in the British Navy. Somers was small, but it was he who supplied the ammunition for Jimmy Quinn in that mighty side of the Edwardian era. So too did Jimmy

McMenemy, but as 'Napoleon' lasted longer, more has been written about him, and the crucial role of Peter Somers has tended to be neglected or underplayed. Like a great many early Celts, Peter died young aged 36 in November 1914, but he remains immortalised nevertheless.

ANDY LYNCH AND 1977

Celtic were going well in 1977 and on Wednesday 13 April at Fir Park, Motherwell, they might well have won the Scottish League. With ten minutes remaining, however, the team were 1–0 down. But then left-back Andy Lynch scored two goals! In other circumstances this would have won the league but unfortunately for Andy and Celtic, they were own goals, and Celtic lost 3–0. Poor Andy had to suffer a certain amount of ridicule about forgetting the teams had changed ends at half time and 'For goodness sake, keep the ball away from Andy, he's after his hat-trick!', but he had the last laugh. Not only was he in the team which won the league at Hibs a few days later, but he also took the penalty kick that won the Scottish Cup that year against Rangers.

THE FRAIL LAD THAT WORE THE GREEN

There was no greater servant for Celtic in the interwar years than Alec Thomson. Alec came from Buckhaven in Fife and joined the club from Wellesley Juniors in 1922. Several years later from the same source came the other Thomson, the goalkeeper John, and indeed the kindly Alec took John under his wing when he arrived at Celtic Park. Alec had started life as a right winger, but it was as an inside right that he made his mark, particularly in the great 5–0 demolition of Rangers in the Scottish Cup semi-final of 1925 when he and Patsy Gallacher dominated the second half. Hard on the heels of that came the glory season of 1925/26 when, as part of the immortal Connolly, Thomson, McGrory, McInally and McLean group, Alec provided great service to the goalscoring talents of Jimmy McGrory and Tommy McInally, and won for himself a Scottish cap in a 1–0 victory over England at Old Trafford in April 1926.

He was a fine passer, a hard worker and a purveyor of the ball, earning himself nicknames like 'Mr Ever Ready' and 'McGrory's fetch and carry man' from a support who soon recognised his worth. His only problem was his slightness of build – he was also called 'the frail lad that wore the green' – and he could be brushed off the ball. Indeed without his false teeth, he looked less that totally intimidating for the opposition, but appearances were deceptive. He was also an unassuming character off the field and possibly lacked a little of the 'devil' necessary to be a top-notch football player. Indeed when he went back to his native Fife in the summer he very soon became 'Eckie Tamson' again, and no-one would realise that he was the great Alec Thomson of Celtic to whom Maley and McGrory owed so much.

It was possibly his unassuming, gentle nature that cost him more Scottish caps. He was a great character in the dressing room, very sympathetic and helpful and trying several times in vain to reconcile the prodigiously talented but self-willed Tommy McInally to the rest of the team. His value was also proved in the events of 1931 when Alec, although himself totally devastated by the death of his friend and namesake

John, proved a strong character to the rest of the team. He managed to win his fourth Scottish Cup medal in 1933 before he departed in 1934 to finish his career with Dunfermline Athletic.

BERWICK RANGERS

There will always be a soft spot in Celtic hearts for Rangers – Berwick Rangers. This is because of the events of 28 January 1967. Celtic were playing Arbroath in the Scottish Cup at Parkhead that day, while Rangers, the Glasgow ones that is, were playing over the border in England at Berwick Rangers, a team whom they had tried to put out of the Scottish League a few years earlier. Berwick had no floodlights, so their game kicked off at 2.45 p.m. in order that the game could thus finish and the supporters' buses could be on their way home in daylight.

In these days, radio coverage was not particularly good in Scotland, although there was a better UK coverage. So no-one really knew for certain what was going on, although rumours circulated that Berwick were winning 1–0. Aye, aye, we thought, they always say this, and the Celtic crowd will always believe such things, for there is no limit to what folk will believe if they want to believe it. It would be nice, mind you . . . but let's just concentrate on the game in hand which Celtic, in their great 1967 style, were winning even though a few good moves from the Arbroath men were eliciting the occasional round of applause.

Celtic, comfortably 3–0 up at half time, were well on top, when suddenly about 15 minutes from the end and for no apparent reason, there was a commotion in the main stand,

and a man with a transistor radio cocked to his ear was seen to signal something to some of the players on the field. The commotion spread throughout the main stand, down to the enclosure, then to the sparsely populated 'Rangers end' of the ground, then to the Jungle and finally to the Celtic End.

'1–0 for Berwick,' everyone said, with even the players getting involved. An Arbroath player was seen to ask what it was all about and when Tommy Gemmell told him, a broad smile appeared on the Arbroath man's face for he was clearly no lover of Rangers.

The ground was now in uproar – but the nagging doubt remained, 'Was it true?'

'It's true, ah tell ye, the English BBC says it.'

'Naw. Ah'm no believin' that!' It would have been cruel if it had all been a hoax, and it was only when the crowd went home and actually saw the result in the evening paper or on TV, that the enormity of it all sunk in.

RELEGATION

Celtic have never been relegated, but 17 April 1948 saw a game at Dens Park in which we came close. In point of fact, defeat in this game would not have relegated them but they would have had to hope that other results went their way. In any case, the cynics believe that somehow or other, Celtic would have been saved by some sort of league reconstruction because it would not have been a good idea to kill a goose that laid one or two fairly large golden eggs as it travelled round the country in the course of a season! It was also rumoured that one or two of the Dundee players might well have, accidentally of course, scored an own goal, if required. The desire of many opposition fans to see Celtic relegated was not of course shared by the clubs themselves.

In any case, 31,000 saw two Celtic men win their spurs that day – Bobby Evans hitherto an average forward, played a brilliant game at right-half and Jock Weir scored a hat-trick, his final goal coming near the end to seal a Celtic victory, celebrated by some supporters as if they had won the Scottish Cup!

GOALKEEPERS ARE WE!

There is a lovely vignette of a game in November 1930 at Celtic Park when Hearts were the visitors. Their goalkeeper Jack Harkness had been the Scotland goalkeeper, but had been unseated by Celtic's John Thomson. Famously chivalrous, at half time (because of the failing daylight, the teams stayed on the field and had a quick cup of tea) Harkness sought out Thomson and the pair of them sat apart from their team-mates. Thus while Maley fulminated at his own team, and Willie McCartney did the same with the Hearts men, the two goalkeepers sat down to discuss the finer points of their craft!

THE THREE THOMSONS OF 1931

Celtic had three Thomsons in 1931 – John, Bertie and Alec. John was the goalkeeper who died so tragically on 5 September 1931, Alec was one of the finest inside forwards

Celtic have ever had, and the least-known of the three was Bertie, a talented winger but also a Glasgow wild boy who, like so many of that age, pressed the self-destruct button, refused to accept the iron discipline of Maley and died only a few months after his 30th birthday in September 1937.

LENNOXTOWN

Situated in the Campsie Hills to the north of Glasgow, this luxurious establishment is Celtic's training centre, and no, it was not named after Bobby Lennox!

CELTIC'S COUNTRY BUMPKIN

Celtic have had no finer servant than the red-faced, bucolic, ungainly looking Peter Wilson from Beith, a man who rejoiced in the nomenclature of 'Celtic's country bumpkin'. He did apparently get himself lost in Woolworth's in Glasgow, so overawed was he by the amount of goods on display, but he never got lost on a football field. For ten years he was one of the mainstays of that charismatic, enchanting but sometimes underperforming Celtic team. At right-half he can be freely be compared to any other of that great Celtic right-halves – and that includes Sunny Jim, Bobby Evans, Pat Crerand and Bobby Murdoch.

'Peter didn't pass the ball – he stroked it,' as Peter's admirers in the *Glasgow Observer* and the *Weekly News* would put it. Peter came into the Celtic team in the chaotic year of 1924, and earned his spurs in a curious incident in a game against

Hearts in October of that year. Celtic had twice missed the same penalty, Patsy Gallacher and Adam McLean being the sinners, but incredibly the referee ordered yet another retake. This time up stepped Peter, casually 'as if he was to take a fork to shovel manure onto a cart' and did the needful. By the end of that season, he had played his part in the two great games which brought the Scottish Cup back to Celtic Park – the 5–0 thumping of Rangers and the 2–1 defeat of Dundee, where his constant supply of long balls had eventually worn down the Dundee defence.

His best season may have been 1925/26 where he was an ever-present as the half-back line of Wilson, McStay and McFarlane dominated the centre of the field and McInally and McGrory did the rest up front, but even when the team did badly, it was noticeable that Wilson seemed to be exempt from the criticism. He won Scottish Cup medals in 1925, 1927, 1931 and 1933, playing a glorious part in all four.

It was perhaps his laid-back nature which prevented him earning more Scottish caps than the four that he did get, but there can be little doubt of his contribution to the cause in the famous beating of England at Hampden in 1933, the day that the Hampden Roar was born. By now, however, he was in the twilight of his Celtic career, playing only sporadically in the disappointing 1933/34 season before leaving to join the sadly under-performing Hibs side of the late 1930s. He was manager of Dunfermline Athletic for a spell, then joined the Royal Navy during the Second World War before retiring to private life as a cabinet maker in Beith. His death in 1983 was greeted with almost personal sadness by those many people who had seen him play and who thought that he was one of the finest players ever to put on a Celtic jersey.

GLASGOW CUP 1908

Celtic were, of course, in 1908, the greatest show on earth. They had won everything in 1907/08 and little seemed able to stop them. But the following autumn, there was a disturbing tendency to draw in the Glasgow Cup so that a lucrative replay was on the cards. Queen's Park had been disposed of after a draw, Rangers had been disposed of, but only after a draw, and when the first game of the Glasgow Cup final against Third Lanark was drawn, supporters and the press were disturbed about the emerging pattern. That game had attracted 40,000. There were 14,000 fewer for the replay the following Saturday for rumours had swept Glasgow that it was going to be another draw. Oh, their prophetic souls! It was indeed another draw and the *Glasgow Herald* was forced to tell everyone how difficult it would be to fix a game, thereby adding to the speculation.

Patience was now wearing thin, and the Glasgow Cup had used up enough Saturdays, so the third game was played on Wednesday 28 October at Celtic Park before a surprisingly large crowd of 18,000 considering it was a Wednesday afternoon. This game was certainly not a draw. It was worse – it was a 4–0 thrashing delivered by an imperious Third Lanark.

What had happened? Did Third Lanark simply play a good game (they were not a bad side at the time)? Or were Celtic indeed 'tired' after too much football, as they unconvincingly tried to say (Weir was out of this game, causing 'Dun' Hay to drop back, and Davie 'Dancer' Hamilton was badly injured after 30 minutes and, of course, there were no substitutes)? Or were there other, darker factors at work? Players' memoirs and reminiscences are curiously silent about this game, and anyone who would know is now long dead, but questions remain, as indeed they do about the Scottish Cup finals of 1926 and 1956. Whatever happened it is a sad blot on the proud records of Adams; McNair and Hay; Young, Loney and Mitchell; Kivlichan, McMenemy, Quinn, Somers and Hamilton. Let's just say it was a bad day, shall we?

SUNNY JIM

A fair-haired right-back commonly known as 'Sunny Jim', James Young was the epitome of the successful Celtic sides of the pre-First World War era. He played for Kilmarnock, Barrow and Bristol Rovers before becoming homesick in Bristol and asking a Celtic representative (who was in the south-west city to sign Bobby Muir) if he could come back to Scotland. This was in spring 1903 and very soon after joining the club he won a Glasgow Charity Cup medal as centre-half. It was, however, as right-half that he would make his name and as part of the half-back lines of Young, Loney and Hay, then Young, Johnstone and McMaster, he dominated Scottish football from 1904 until his retirement through injury in 1917. He played a mighty part in the performances of the team which won six league championships in a row from 1905 until 1910. He was captain of Celtic from 1911 onwards, but only won one Scottish cap against Ireland in 1906, although he played six times for the Scottish League.

He was a natural leader and always seemed to enjoy the confidence of Willie Maley who had a high regard for him, but his outspokenness did not always endear him to others, and this may explain why he was so under-capped by Scotland. He was, however, totally committed to the Celtic cause with his fine play, grim determination and his inspirational style of leadership. Even when his fellow Ayrshireman Jimmy Hay was still captain, Young's broad, raucous Ayrshire accent was heard in every ground he played, advising, encouraging and cajoling his team-mates. 'Face the ball, Celts!' became his war cry. He was capable of dishing out the raw meat as well – on one famous occasion at Forfar in February 1914 he earned a belt over the head from the umbrella of the mother of a player whom he had repeatedly fouled. Yet he remained perpetually cheerful and jovial, well-deserving of the nickname 'Sunny Jim', the name of a character in a newspaper advertisement who ate all his breakfast cereal.

> 'Vigour, Vim, Perfect Trim
> That's why we call him Sunny Jim!'

Lucky enough to have a job in a reserved occupation during the war, he played on for Celtic until a nasty knee injury on 30 September 1916 effectively ended his career and obliged him to walk with a permanent limp. He returned to his native Ayrshire to become the host of the George Hotel, Kilmarnock. He met his death in a motorcycle accident on 4 September 1922, at the age of only 40, and he is buried in the Grassyards Cemetery, Kilmarnock. In the opinion of Eugene MacBride, who wrote the massive work *An Alphabet of the Celts,* Sunny Jim is the greatest Celt of all time.

BRITISH LEAGUE CUP

Otherwise known as the Glasgow Exhibition Trophy, or the Coronation Cup, the British League Cup was a one-off tournament held in 1902 for the Ibrox Disaster Fund. Rangers had won the Glasgow Exhibition Trophy in 1901, and put up this cup for the first-ever British tournament between themselves, Celtic, Sunderland and Everton, the champions and runners-up in each country. The Ibrox Disaster Fund would benefit, and the winners could claim to be the best in Britain. By coincidence, the tournament was played in the run-up to the coronation of King Edward VII, and is sometimes referred to as the Coronation Cup, but it should not be confused with that of 1953.

Celtic beat Sunderland 5–1 at Celtic Park on 30 April 1902 with two goals from Tommy McDermott and one each from the old faithful left-wing partnership of Sandy McMahon and Johnny Campbell. After a draw at Goodison, Rangers beat Everton on 3 May at Celtic Park, the venue determined by Ibrox still being out of commission.

Cathkin was the venue for the final between Celtic and Rangers on 17 June 1902. The late date of this game can be explained by the desire to have the game played as close as possible to the coronation of King Edward VII, which was scheduled for 26 June. (In the event, King Edward VII took ill with appendicitis and the coronation had to be postponed until 9 August.) The receipts from this final were a very healthy £314, and it took a late header from Jimmy Quinn, in the last minute of extra time, to decide the issue. Celtic had gone two goals ahead through Jimmy Quinn, but before half time Bob Hamilton had taken full advantage of a goalkeeping fumble to reduce the leeway, then Finlay Speedie equalised for Rangers. The second half saw no further scoring, and when full time came many of the public and the press had gone home, assuming that there would be a replay. But both teams agreed to extra time of ten minutes each way, and Jimmy Quinn scored at the very end. The line-ups were, Celtic: McPherson, Watson, Battles, Loney, Marshall, Orr, Crawford, Campbell, Quinn, McDermott, Hamilton. Rangers: Dickie, N. Smith, Crawford, Gibson, Stark, Robertson, Lennie, Walker, Hamilton, Speedie, A. Smith. This triumph was much celebrated by Celtic fans:

> Some say the Rangers are guid at fitba'
> Wi' Speedie, Gibson and Lennie an a'
> But Jimmy Quinn, he diddled them a'
> At the Glasgow Exhibition oh!

However, it was very much a Celtic team in transition. They had disappointed their fans by losing the Scottish League and the Scottish Cup in 1902, and the great Celtic team of a few years later had still to assemble.

CORONATION CUP

This was a competition held in Glasgow to commemorate the coronation of Queen Elizabeth II in 1953. It was decided by both the English and the Scottish authorities that four teams from each country should be invited to take part. Newcastle United, Arsenal (English league champions), Manchester United and Tottenham Hotspur accepted the invitation, as did Hibernian, Rangers (Scottish League and Scottish Cup winners), Celtic and Aberdeen. Blackpool, the winners of the FA Cup, did not take part, nor did Preston North End or Wolves, who finished second and third respectively in the English league. The Glasgow grounds of Hampden Park and Ibrox were chosen because it was felt that London would be too busy with the coronation itself. Celtic Park would have been big enough but in 1953 the facilities lagged behind those of the other two Glasgow grounds.

The teams chosen were considered to be the best available crowd-pullers and Celtic, who had had a poor season, finishing eighth in the Scottish League, were invited to take part only because of the size of their following and the fact that all games were to be played in Glasgow. Yet they ended up the winners in an epic final against Hibs, in which Johnny Bonnar, the Celtic goalkeeper, aided by captain Jock Stein, famously defied Hibs'' Famous Five' forward line. The whole competition was a pleasant surprise for Scottish teams, particularly Hibs and Celtic, and was well attended throughout. The irony, however, of the Coronation Cup final being played on an occasion when 'all Hampden was covered in green, white and gold' rather than the red, white and blue which one might have expected, was not lost on supporters of Celtic and Hibernian. The triumph was celebrated with street parties and 'dancing in the streets of the Gorbals'.

Celtic beat Arsenal in the quarter-final at Hampden on 11 May before 59,538 fans through a Bobby Collins goal, while in the other games, Hibs beat Tottenham Hotspur, Manchester United beat Rangers and Newcastle United beat Aberdeen. 73,466 then came to Hampden to see Celtic, with goals from Bertie Peacock and Neil Mochan, beat Manchester United 2–1 while in the other semi-final, Hibs put Newcastle United to the sword and beat them 4–0.

The final was played on a very pleasant summer evening before a crowd given as 117,060, but with many more locked out of Hampden when the gates were closed, as the east terracing was dangerously overcrowded. Hibs, the form team, who had only narrowly lost the Scottish League on goal average, were expected to win. In addition Hibs had demolished Newcastle United in the semi-final with a breathtaking display of attacking football – but Celtic, strengthened by new signing Neil Mochan, who compensated for the absence of the injured Tully, scored first, then resisted the intense onslaught of the Hibs forward line throughout the second half until a breakaway led to another and decisive goal for Celtic.

> And alas for the hopes of our true royal blues
> The Celtic beat Manchester and Arsenal too
> The Hibs in the final, all lo and behold!
> All Hampden was covered in green, white and gold!

Celtic: Bonnar, Haughney, Rollo, Evans, Stein, McPhail, Collins, Walsh, Mochan, Peacock, Fernie.

Hibs: Younger, Govan, Paterson, Buchanan, Howie, Combe, Smith, Johnstone, Reilly, Turnbull, Ormond.
The referee was H. Phillips from Wishaw.

LEIGH ROOSE

This remarkable goalkeeper, an amateur who had played for Wales against Scotland at Kilmarnock the week before, played one game for Celtic – and it was a very unfortunate one as

Celtic, without Sunny Jim Young and Jimmy McMenemy and of course goalkeeper Davie Adams, went down 3–1 to Clyde at Shawfield in a Scottish Cup semi-final. Leigh distinguished himself by running after Jackie Chalmers when he had scored the third goal for Clyde and shaking him by the hand! This amiable gentleman then returned to Sunderland. Tragically he was killed at the Somme in October 1916.

THE BROTHERS MALEY

Willie Maley had three brothers, two of whom played a part in Scottish football. The elder brother Tom, of course, played in Celtic's first game and at the end of his career became a manager. In 1904 the Maley brothers, as managers, won the Scottish and English Cups. Willie watched Jimmy Quinn score the hat-trick that won the Scottish Cup final on 16 April 1904, and the following week was at the Crystal Palace to see his brother Tom's Manchester City beat Bolton Wanderers 1–0 in the English FA Cup final. Tom was sacked from Manchester City in 1906 after an illegal payment scandal but later became manager of Bradford Park Avenue. One of the things he did was to introduce a new strip for Bradford – green and white horizontal stripes! He did a great deal for Celtic on the administrative side, and was widely believed to have been the mystery journalist of the *Glasgow Observer* who was known as 'Man In The Know'.

On two occasions Willie Maley faced his younger brother Alec as manager in a Scottish Cup final. One was in 1912 when Alec was manager of Clyde, and the other was in 1923 when Alec had moved on to manage Hibs. On both occasions Willie and Celtic emerged triumphant. Alec was also reputed to have been the man who rescued the Scottish Cup from the mob on the occasion of the Hampden Riot in 1909.

TOMMY DUFF THE GOALIE

Celtic had no league or cup game on New Year's Day 1892 and thus arranged a friendly against Dumbarton so that they could pioneer their goal nets. A few 'fringe' players were given a game as well, including goalkeeper Tommy Duff who had played for a few other teams, notably Cowlairs. He had suffered from rheumatism (a common complaint in Victorian Britain) and was on medication for it. He should not have taken alcohol while he was on such medication, but New Year being New Year, could not resist doing so. The result was that he turned up for the game less than 100 per cent focussed and gave a performance which was 'mediocre in the extreme' according to the *Glasgow Observer,* and the team lost 8–0 to the emphatic Sons of the Rock. It was of course no disgrace to lose a game to Dumbarton (then current Scottish champions) but 8–0 was a bit much, especially when the real reason for Duff's poor performance became obvious. Some supporters thought that it was because he was a Protestant or even an Orangeman that he had played so poorly, but the truth was a little more basic. At least the deployment of goal nets at Old Celtic Park prevented anyone from having to run after the ball on eight occasions (or actually eleven, because the referee, compassionate and kind-hearted, chalked off another three).

EMPIRE EXHIBITION TROPHY

In 38 there was a show
Glasgow was the place to go
A model of the tower was football's prize.
England sent four of the best
They didn't meet with much successful
For the trophy ended up in Paradise!

This was a one-off tournament, played between four leading sides of Scotland and four leading sides of England, in late May and early June 1938, to commemorate the Empire Exhibition being held at Bellahouston Park, Glasgow. The exhibition was to be 'an exposition of the work, life, culture and progress' of the British Empire, and was a much-needed propaganda counterblast to what was coming from Nazi Germany. As Glasgow (the 'Second City of the Empire') was frequently described as the football capital of the world, it was felt that a football tournament between eight invited sides would be a fitting part of the 'work, culture, life and progress' of Glasgow. A trophy was commissioned in the image of the Tait Tower, the symbol of the Empire Exhibition. All the games were played at Ibrox, because of its proximity to Bellahouston Park. Sadly, neither Arsenal (the English league winners) nor Preston North End (the FA Cup winners) took part, but the tournament was still hotly contested, and the winners could claim to be the champions of Britain.

Celtic needed a replay to dispose of Sunderland in the quarter-final (3–1 with goals from Johnny Crum and two from John Divers), while Aberdeen, Hearts and Everton were the other winners. Johnny Crum also scored against Hearts in the semi-final (the only goal of the game) before 52,000 fans while Everton squeezed narrowly past Aberdeen.

The final between Celtic and Everton was an epic between two great teams. 'Fetch a polis man, Everton's getting murdered,' was the cry of the Celtic fans before the game, but the reality was quite different, for the game was tight and hard-fought, with a winner possible at either end. Celtic had Jimmy Delaney back from injury and his presence was probably crucial, although it was Johnny Crum who broke the deadlock when he scored the only goal of the game after seven minutes of extra time. Famously, he then ran behind the goal and did a 'Highland fling' for the benefit of the fans. He had thus scored in every round. The second half of the game and the extra time was broadcast on radio on the BBC Regional Service, beginning at 7.50 p.m., and the commentator was the *Sunday Mail* journalist Rex Kingsley. Johnny Crum, the hero of the hour, was married the following Wednesday.

It was a triumph much celebrated by Celtic fans, and it is a mystery why the team did not go forward from there. The club's Golden Jubilee was celebrated a few days later, and it was confidently expected that the ageing Maley would announce his retirement but he failed to do so. The club then had a terrible season in 1938/39 and played through the Second World War with a distinct lack of success, and it was 1951 before a major Scottish honour was again won. So, although this was a great triumph, it also heralded the start of Celtic's darkest days.

Celtic: Kennaway, Hogg, Morrison, Geatons, Lyon, Paterson, Delaney, MacDonald, Crum, Divers, Murphy.

Everton: Sagar, Cook, Greenhalgh, Mercer, Jones, Thomson, Geldard, Cunliffe, Lawton, Stevenson, Boyes.
The referee was T. Thomson from Northumberland.

THE O'DONNELL BROTHERS

Not to be confused with Phil O'Donnell who played for
Celtic in the 1990s, Frank and Hugh O'Donnell played in
Celtic's team in the 1930s. They were born in Buckhaven in
Fife in 1911 and 1915 respectively. Frank, the elder brother
was a centre forward and Hugh, the younger brother, was an
outside left. Hugh won a Scottish Cup medal in 1933, but it
was probably true to say that neither was a total success at
Celtic Park as both were transferred to Preston North End
at the end of the 1935 season. Both were in the Preston team
which lost 3–1 to Sunderland in the English FA Cup final of
1937 but Hugh was more successful when he won an FA Cup
medal in 1938 when Preston beat Huddersfield 1–0. Frank
won six caps for Scotland.

SCOTTISH LEAGUE

Whether we mean the Scottish Football League or the
Scottish Premier League (from 1998/99) Celtic's record is
a disappointing one with only 43 wins, some 11 less than
Rangers. The cause is probably that Celtic have a tendency
to play the better and more attractive football, but often
lack the consistency to win mundane games at places like
Falkirk, Airdrie and in latter years, Inverness. So often 'we
threw away the league' has been the cry, and Rangers have
become champions by default. It is certainly true that if Celtic
do not challenge Rangers, no-one else will, for although
Hearts, Hibs, Aberdeen and the two Dundee clubs have had
their moments, they tend (as Celtic do on occasion) to be like

rabbits trapped in a car's headlights and believe that Rangers have some sort of divine right to win. Other than Celtic or Rangers, no team has been champions of Scotland since 1985.

On the other hand, Celtic have had their great periods, notably the six-in-a-row from 1905 until 1910, the four-in-a-row from 1914 until 1917, the nine-in-a-row from 1966 until 1974 and the three-in-a-row in more recent times from 2006 until 2008. The most convincing victory of the Scottish League was in 2002 when with 103 points, they were 18 points clear of Rangers and clinched the title on 6 April in a 5–1 defeat of Livingston. On four occasions since the turn of the century Celtic have suffered the agony of losing the league on the last day, the most notorious being 'Black Sunday' in 2005 when, leading 1–0 against Motherwell, they lost two late goals and gifted the title to an undeserving Rangers.

The most dramatic Scottish League win must surely be 1909 when Celtic played eight games in twelve days to pip Dundee. And all this happened after the traumatic Hampden Riot at the 1909 Scottish Cup final! 1986 is a worthy rival to this one, however, for on the last day, Celtic had to beat St Mirren by four clear goals and hope that Dundee could beat Hearts at Dens Park. In circumstances that can barely be imagined, this actually happened for Celtic beat St Mirren 5–0 at Love Street while the supporters lapsed into introverted silence reflecting what could have been . . . until the crackling transistors brought the news from BBC Radio Scotland that Dundee had scored, then scored again at Dens Park.

Celtic's 43 victories in this competition came in 1893, 1894, 1896, 1898, 1905, 1906, 1907, 1908, 1909, 1910, 1914, 1915, 1916, 1917, 1919, 1922, 1926, 1936, 1938, 1954, 1966, 1967, 1968, 1969, 1970, 1971, 1972, 1973, 1974, 1977, 1979, 1981, 1982, 1986, 1988, 1998, 2001, 2002, 2004, 2006, 2007, 2008 and 2012.

GREAT MEN DO GREAT THINGS

On a cold and frosty day at Parkhead in December 1969, Kilmarnock's Frank Beattie was injured on the hard ground and looked to have broken his leg. He was a player much respected by opponents, and Parkhead was hushed before a ripple of applause broke out as he was stretchered off. Jock Stein, visibly upset at the horrific injury to a fine player, took off his overcoat and laid it over Frank as he passed the dugout.

SCOTTISH LEAGUE CUP

This tournament had its genesis in the Second World War as the Southern League Cup and was first played for officially in the 1946/47 season. Celtic have won the trophy fourteen times but trail woefully behind Rangers in the list of the winners. Although there have been some great performances, notably the famous 7–1 demolition of Rangers in 1957 and the unequalled five-in-a-row between 1965 and 1969, there has probably been more heartache than joy in the Scottish League Cup. The trophy had been in existence for a decade before Celtic won it, and it is a scarcely believable statistic that East Fife had won the trophy three times and Dundee twice before Celtic even appeared in a final! Part of the reason for this was that Celtic were notoriously poor starters to the season and the League Cup usually opened the season in August.

More heartache came for Celtic fans in the 1970s when there was a string of defeats in the final. Four League Cup finals – 1964, 1986, 1990 and 2011 – saw a Celtic team play better than Rangers but nevertheless lose the game. There were many woefully weak performances on autumn evenings when teams like Dundee United, Falkirk, Aberdeen and Hearts could hardly believe their luck, and for a supporter, the worst of them all was surely the final at Ibrox in November 1994 when, with Celtic at a low ebb and craving a trophy after years of deprivation, neglect and incompetent management, Tommy Burns' team contrived to lose to First Division Raith Rovers in a penalty shoot-out!

Nevertheless, there has been happiness as well, and the fourteen occasions on which the League Cup has returned in triumph to Parkhead are as follows:

Celtic 3–0 Partick Thistle, Hampden, 31 October 1956

McPhail (2), Collins

This game was played with an afternoon kick-off on a Wednesday (Hampden would not have floodlights for several years yet) with Great Britain on the brink of war during the Suez Crisis. Celtic's goals all came in the early part of the second half, and Celtic ran out comfortable winners after an appalling performance in the first game which Thistle really should have won.

Celtic 7–1 Rangers, Hampden, 19 October 1957

McPhail (3), Mochan (2), Wilson, Fernie (penalty)

One of the great games in Celtic's history. The scoreline says it all really, but after this game, the dark days descended with a vengeance.

Celtic 2–1 Rangers, Hampden, 23 October 1965

Hughes (2 penalties)

The game which confirmed that Jock Stein's Celtic had arrived. John Hughes ('Yogi Bear'), whose temperament had been suspect up until now, showed commendable coolness in sinking the two penalties, but the real hero was goalkeeper Ronnie Simpson who showed all the experience in the world during Rangers' late onslaught.

Celtic 1–0 Rangers, Hampden, 29 October 1966

Lennox

A tight game made memorable by the 'three-card trick' goal of Auld taking a free kick finding the head of McBride who nodded the ball down to the onrushing Lennox, and the fine goal-line clearance in the second half by Willie O'Neill.

Celtic 5–3 Dundee, Hampden, 28 October 1967

Chalmers (2), Hughes, Lennox, Wallace

A goalscoring feast for which Dundee deserve an equal amount of credit. Both teams were given a deserved ovation at the end.

Celtic 6–2 Hibs, Hampden, 5 April 1969

Lennox (3), Wallace, Auld, Craig

A vintage Celtic performance, arguably one of the best of the Stein era for sheer breathtaking football.

Celtic 1–0 St Johnstone, Hampden, 25 October 1969

Auld

This was St Johnstone's first ever national cup final, but they were by no means overawed, and indeed but for a few saves from John Fallon near the end, the Perth men might well have equalised Bertie Auld's early goal.

Celtic 6–3 Hibs, Hampden, 26 October 1974

Deans (3), Johnstone, Wilson, Murray

A fine performance bringing to an end a depressing run of League Cup final defeats. Joe Harper, never exactly the darling of the Parkhead crowd, was given a sympathetic reception for accomplishing what might well be a unique feat in world football, namely scoring a hat-trick yet finishing up on the losing side in a cup final.

Celtic 2–1 Rangers, Hampden, 4 December 1982

Nicholas, MacLeod

A much-needed boost for Celtic to win this game played in December, in the rain, in a stadium that was in the throes of being renovated. Why was a final played in such circumstances? Celtic were on top throughout even after Rangers pulled a goal back in the second half.

Celtic 3–0 Dundee United, Ibrox, 30 November 1997

Rieper, Larsson, Burley

Celtic ended fifteen years of disappointing under-achievement in this tournament with a competent and relaxed demolition of the Tannadice men. It was the first trophy success for Wim Jansen and tangible proof that Celtic meant business in their quest to win the league championship.

Celtic 2–0 Aberdeen, Hampden, 19 March 2000

Riseth, Johnson

This game was a much-needed boost to Celtic fans who had just experienced the humiliation of going out of the Scottish Cup to Inverness. Caretaker-manager Kenny Dalglish did well, for this was a poor Celtic side defeating an Aberdeen team which similarly had seen better times.

Celtic 3–0 Kilmarnock, Hampden, 18 March 2001

Larsson (3)

Martin O'Neill's first trophy for Celtic, who were struggling with injury, suspension and non-availability of players. Celtic played a large part of the second half without Chris Sutton who had been dismissed, but Henrik Larsson's hat-trick was a joy to behold.

Celtic 3–0 Dunfermline, Hampden, 19 March 2006

Zurawski, Maloney, Dublin

Gordon Strachan's first trophy for Celtic, but the victory had been won a month previously when Celtic beat the Pars 9–0 at East End Park in an SPL match. Dunfermline were delighted to keep Celtic to three in this game! Dion Dublin had a long and distinguished career with quite a few clubs, but this was his only medal, and he scored the last goal.

Celtic 2–0 Rangers (after extra time), Hampden, 15 March 2009

O'Dea, McGeady (penalty)

A game which Celtic should have won by more goals than they did with Darren O'Dea being the unlikely scorer of the first goal early in extra time.

Celtic have had four men who have scored hat-tricks in Scottish League Cup finals – Billy McPhail, Bobby Lennox, Dixie Deans and Henrik Larsson.

GLASGOW CHARITY CUP

This tournament, originally known as the Glasgow Merchants' Charity Cup, is no longer played for, a fact that many Scottish football fans regard as a shame. It is the second-oldest trophy in Scottish football, having been launched in 1876/77 by Glasgow merchants to raise money for charities, and it served that purpose for many decades. Until 1961 it was competed for at the end of every season (including war years) by Glasgow clubs, although on special occasions like the aftermath of the Ibrox disaster of 1902, teams from outside the city were invited to compete.

Even with the arrival of professionalism in the 1890s, it was expected that the players would provide their services free, although some observers suspected that they did not always do so. The tournament was taken seriously but, being played at the end of the season, it lacked the status of the Scottish Cup or even the Glasgow Cup. By 1961 the month of May, when the Charity Cup was usually held, was becoming crowded with overseas tours, international fixtures and a later finish to the season, and clubs were withdrawing from the competition. The device of 'counting corners' was used to decide a winner so that a replay would not be necessary, and the trophy was shared on two occasions in latter years. After 1960/61 the tournament was abandoned but the magnificent trophy now resides in the museum at Hampden Park.

Celtic won the trophy on 27 occasions in 1892, 1893, 1894, 1895, 1896, 1899, 1903, 1905, 1908, 1912, 1913, 1914, 1915, 1916, 1917, 1918, 1920, 1921, 1924, 1926, 1936, 1937, 1938, 1943, 1950, 1953, 1959 and shared it with Clyde in 1961. The 1892 Charity Cup final was the last game ever played on Old Celtic Park, and the 1936 Charity Cup final was the famous one in which Delaney scored a hat-trick against Rangers and instead of smiles and congratulations from Maley was told grimly, 'Don't let that go to your head!'

GLASGOW CUP

This competition, with its magnificent Victorian trophy, is no longer competed for by senior clubs, but in its heyday it was much prized and valued, next to the Scottish Cup. It came into being when the SFA ruled in 1887 that teams like Queen's Park and Rangers could no longer take part in the English FA Cup as well as the Scottish Cup. The loss of English Cup revenue was a serious one, and to offset this, and to prevent the whole season being nothing other than the Scottish Cup and meaningless friendlies, a new trophy was provided for Glasgow clubs. Because of seniority (it is three years older than the Scottish League) it was able to claim precedence about fixtures, and the final tended to be played in October, usually the autumn Glasgow holiday weekend. The competition was played for during both wars (unlike the Scottish Cup), mainly because it involved few transport problems. After the Second World War, the appearance of the Scottish League Cup removed the Glasgow Cup from its autumn slot, and eventually the tournament disappeared altogether under pressure from increasing European and international fixtures. Yet as late as 1966/67 in Celtic's *annus mirabilis*, the club were proud to claim the Glasgow Cup as one of the five trophies that they entered and won. In the following year, 1968, Rangers withdrew from the tournament, claiming fixture congestion, which allowed Celtic fans to describe their decision as 'cowardice'. It was a decision that would rebound on Rangers because on 17 April while Celtic were defeating Clyde 8–0 at Hampden to win the Glasgow Cup, Rangers lost a vital point at Greenock which would give Celtic the initiative in the Scottish League race. Celtic won the competition 28 times.

In 1891 Celtic actually won the trophy twice, on 14 February and 12 December, but it was in two separate seasons with the victory in February being Celtic's first real major trophy. 28 September 1940 was possibly when the Glasgow Cup that meant the most to their supporters as Celtic beat Rangers 1–0 at a time when London was being blitzed and it was expected that the same was about to happen to Glasgow. It was a rare wartime triumph for Celtic, and meant a huge amount for those who were about to go overseas.

Celtic's victories were in 1890/01, 1891/92, 1894/95, 1895/96, 1904/05, 1905/06, 1906/07, 1907/08, 1909/10, 1915/16, 1916/17, 1919/20, 1920/21, 1926/27, 1927/28, 1928/29, 1930/31, 1938/39, 1940/41, 1948/49, 1955/56, 1961/62, 1963/64, 1964/65, 1966/67, 1967/68, 1969/70 and 1981/82.

EUROPEAN CUP/ CHAMPIONS LEAGUE

Everyone knows that Celtic won the European Cup in 1967. Glory be to the immortal Lisbon Lions of Simpson, Craig and Gemmell; Murdoch, McNeill and Clark; Johnstone, Wallace, Chalmers, Auld and Lennox who on 25 May 1967 beat Inter Milan 2–1 with goals from Gemmell and Chalmers to become the first British team and to date the only Scottish team to have done so.

> Well fourteen years had passed and so
> To Portugal we had to go
> To play the team that Italy adored.
> Celtic went out to attack

They won the big Cup and they brought it back
The first time it had been on British shores!

No words of praise are too extravagant for manager Jock Stein and these men who beat Zurich, Nantes, Vojvodina and Dukla Prague on the way to the final and completed a clean sweep of domestic honours that year as well. Sadly, however, it has been difficult to replicate that success. In 1970 Celtic reached the final only to lose disappointingly to Feyenoord in a game for which Celtic were firm favourites but simply did not perform on the night, presumably taking the opposition too lightly following their epic defeat of Leeds United in the semi-final. On two other occasions in the early 1970s, Celtic reached the semi-finals, losing in a heart-breaking penalty shoot-out in 1972 to Inter Milan, and having the misfortune to be kicked off the park by a thuggish Atlético Madrid in 1974.

Since then, it has been heartbreak all the way in Europe with the team seldom being in Europe after Christmas. There have been the odd moments of success and euphoria – Real Madrid, AC Milan and Manchester United have all been defeated at Parkhead, for example – but away form has been shocking. The question is often asked, given the amount of money that is in the game in England and Spain for example, is it possible for Celtic (or any Scottish team) to compete meaningfully in Europe again? Those of us who recall 1967 will refuse to believe that it is not possible and recall the words of the old song, 'We've done it before and we'll do it again!'

THREE UNHAPPY NEW YEARS IN A ROW

It would be no great surprise if Celtic fans old enough to recall the early 1960s have a complex about the New Year. 1963 saw the appalling 4–0 collapse at Ibrox when there was dressing room dissension; 1964 at Parkhead saw genuine hard luck with Celtic, denied a penalty and missing several chances, going down 1–0 to a fortunate Rangers side; and 1965 at Ibrox was the worst of all with Celtic at a low ebb but playing well enough to win – and would have done so if Jimmy Johnstone had not been sent off towards the end of the first half, and Bobby Murdoch had not missed a penalty towards the end of the second half. It was painful!

EUROPEAN CUP WINNERS' CUP

This now-defunct competition (for the winners of the national cup competition in each country) provided Celtic with many exciting moments and fine performances but bad luck was the key factor on at least two occasions. In 1963/64 Celtic (they were actually the defeated finalist of the Scottish Cup in 1963 but allowed in because Rangers were playing in the European Cup) reached the semi-final against the Hungarian team MTK. Playing superb football they beat MTK 3–0 at Parkhead in the first leg and looked odds-on for the final. But their outlook and preparation were naïve in two respects. They kept on attacking recklessly and foolishly when they did not need to, and they also came to grief when they expected fair play in Hungary from an Austrian referee.

Celtic, to the distress of their supporters listening on the radio back home, went down 4–0.

Then two years later in 1965/66 an absolute howler of a decision defeated Celtic at Liverpool in the semi-final. Celtic, 1–0 up from the first leg at Parkhead, lost two goals at Anfield but then Bobby Lennox ran past Ron Yeats to score an equaliser only to discover that he had been flagged for offside by a linesman who clearly could not credit the speed of Lennox.

1984/85 was the Rapid Vienna fiasco which really can only be described in terms of sheer cheating, and then the following year Celtic were compelled to play their game against Atlético Madrid behind closed doors.

And then we come to the tragic events of 1989 when Partizan Belgrade came to Parkhead 2–1 up from the first leg. Celtic played magnificently, scored five goals (with Dziekanowski scoring four of them) and seemed to have the game won, and then with the massive Parkhead crowd in an uproar, lost a soft goal and went out on the away goals rule! 'There ought to be a law against what Celtic do to their supporters!' said a neutral observer.

NOT THAT WE'RE PARANOID

Celtic fans are often accused of having a chip on their shoulders about referees. It's not true, of course, but before anyone becomes too self-righteous, it's perhaps an idea to consider the events at Ibrox on 7 January 1978. Celtic were a goal down, and were denied a blatant penalty by referee J.R.P. Gordon of Newport-on-Tay when Joe Craig was pushed in the back. While Celtic players were protesting and were still in the Rangers penalty area, Rangers were allowed to take a quick goal kick (illegal because there were still Celtic players in the penalty box), then ran up the field and scored against Celtic's depleted defence! At this point mayhem naturally erupted with Celtic players threatening to walk off in protest until persuaded to do otherwise by trainer Neil Mochan and manager Jock Stein. Rangers went on to win 3–1, but it is games like this that make even the most moderate of people begin to wonder about the probity of referees! Things were not helped by the subsequent revelation of Mr Gordon's support of Rangers, and his accepting of 'gifts of hospitality' on a European trip.

INTER CITIES FAIRS CUP/ UEFA CUP/EUROPA LEAGUE

This tournament, under whatever guise one cares to call it, has been pretty dreadful for Celtic and really should be passed over. There is however one exception and that is 2003 when Celtic reached the final in Seville to lose to José Mourinho's FC Porto with a goalkeeping error and the ending off of Bobo Balde contributing to the narrow defeat and cancelling out the two excellent headed goals by Henrik Larsson. There were positives, however, for Celtic in that the fans were there in strength and behaved impeccably winning plaudits and awards for so doing (the behaviour of the fans of another Scottish club in Manchester in similar circumstances some five years later was a lot less praiseworthy) and the road to Seville was littered with some excellent team performances not least in the removal of two English clubs in Blackburn Rovers (managed by Graeme Souness) and Liverpool.

HUDDLE

Believed to have been started by Tony Mowbray when he played in the 1994/95 season, this is now an iconic phenomenon wherever Celtic play, before the start of a game. It has of course been slavishly copied by other teams, and in recent seasons it has spread to the support as well, thanks to the pioneering of the 'Green Brigade'. The support now all turn their back on the game for a moment and jump up and down in unison to chants like 'Let's All Do the Huddle', etc. There are few more awe-inspiring sights in world football, showing as it does the unique bond between players and supporters at Celtic.

MANAGERS

Celtic have had eighteen managers (if we wish to count Billy McNeill twice) since 1897. Before 1897, the word 'manager' does not apply because the team was selected by a committee. Even in 1897, Maley was appointed secretary/manager and in theory at least had no power to choose the team. In fact, such was his energy, ability and charm, Maley made most decisions at the club. Jimmy McGrory quite clearly did not have total control of team selection, but when Jock Stein was appointed in 1965 he insisted on total control of such matters and subsequent managers have enjoyed similar power.

Willie Maley	1897–1940
Jimmy McStay	1940–5
Jimmy McGrory	1945–65

Jock Stein	1965–78
Billy McNeill	1978–83
Davie Hay	1983–7
Billy McNeill	1987–91
Liam Brady	1991–3
Lou Macari	1993–4
Tommy Burns	1994–7
Wim Jansen	1997–8
Jozef Vengloš	1998–9
John Barnes	1999–2000
Kenny Dalglish	2000 (February – May)
Martin O'Neill	2001–5
Gordon Strachan	2005–9
Tony Mowbray	2009–10
Neil Lennon	2010–

In terms of success, most Celtic historians would place Jock Stein first, Willie Maley second and Martin O'Neill third.

FOUR AWFUL SCOTTISH CUP FINALS

Between their Scottish Cup successes of 1954 and 1965, Celtic lost four Scottish Cup finals three of which went to replays – Clyde in 1955, Hearts in 1956, Dunfermline in 1961 and Rangers in 1963. In all four cases Celtic supporters left Hampden puzzled and upset, but a common factor in all four cases was faulty team selection – in 1955 Bobby Collins was dropped for the replay; in 1956 Mike Haughney, an excellent full-back, was played at inside right and a youngster called Billy Craig was played on the right wing.

In 1961, even after Jim Kennedy went down with appendicitis the club failed to recall the experienced Bertie Peacock from a meaningless Northern Ireland friendly and in 1963 wingers Jimmy Johnstone and Frank Brogan, who had played so well in the first game against Rangers, were dropped for the replay.

There were other factors as well. The 1956 final was the one which did not go to a replay as Celtic were well beaten 3–1 by a good Hearts team but questions continue to be asked about the performance of certain key players. In 1955 the first game might have been won but for an unfortunate goalkeeping error at a corner kick. In 1961, Celtic simply underestimated the vitality of Jock Stein's Dunfermline and 15 May 1963 remains one of Celtic's saddest ever nights as Hampden was treated to the astonishing sight of 50,000 Celtic fans leaving the ground en masse with about 25 minutes to go as Rangers scored their third goal against an underperforming Celtic team.

MESSAGE TO THE VATICAN

Celtic's first really great season was 1892 when the team won the Glasgow Cup, the Scottish Cup and the Glasgow Charity Cup. This was all too much for committee man Ned McGinn who sent a message to the Vatican asking His Holiness if he would like to burn some candles in honour of this achievement. As fas as anyone can discover, His Holiness did not comply.

HELLO! HELLO!

Commonly believed to be a Rangers song, but it was Celtic who had it first! It was of course originally a song called 'Marching Through Georgia' from the American Civil War and was a triumphalist paean of Abraham Lincoln's Northern armies as they set the slaves free. But in March 1925 Celtic unexpectedly beat Rangers 5–0 in the Scottish Cup semi-final with Patsy Gallacher, Alec Thomson and Jimmy McGrory all at their best, and the Celtic supporters sang about this for the next forty years.

Hello! Hello! We are the Tim Malloys!
Hello! Hello! You'll know us by the noise!
We beat the Rangers in the Cup, 'twas great to be alive
Not one, not two, not three, not four but FIVE!

TOMMY SINCLAIR – CELTIC'S RANGERS GOALIE

A case could be made out for arguing that Celtic best ever goalkeeper was not John Thomson, Charlie Shaw or Ronnie Simpson but Tommy Sinclair in that 88 per cent of his games for Celtic were shut-outs and in the one game that he played that was not a shut-out, he won a medal! Not only that, but he was actually a Rangers player on loan at the time!

These remarkable events occurred at the start of the 1906/07 season when Celtic's goalkeeper Davie Adams cut his hand badly on a nail sticking out of a goalpost at Ibrox during a benefit match for a Rangers player. Rangers were upset about this and manager William Wilton (being the nice man that he was) offered his friend Willie Maley the services of their reserve goalkeeper Tommy Sinclair until Adams' hand healed up. Sinclair was very happy about this for it gave him first-team football and he was in any case a good friend of Alec Bennett and Jimmy McMenemy with whom he had played at Rutherglen Glencairn.

Tommy duly played the first nine games of the 1906/07 season. In truth he had little to do other than watch Jimmy Quinn score fourteen goals at the other end, for Celtic had a superb side winning their first six league games and reaching the Glasgow Cup final without losing a goal, with Sinclair dealing superbly with whatever came his way.

But in the Glasgow Cup final on 6 October 1906, although Celtic won, two goals were conceded to the chagrin of the likeable Tommy who was however much mollified by the award of a medal. That game was also the first game that season in which Jimmy Quinn had NOT scored for Celtic, so presumably Jimmy was equally upset.

Davie Adams returned the following week, and Tommy was on his reluctant way back to Ibrox where he once again failed to get a first team place. Near the end of the season, he was transferred to Newcastle United for whom he played a few games in their triumphant capture of the English League Championship. Tommy could therefore feel that he contributed to the winning of the league championship in both countries! And of course, he had a Glasgow Cup medal as well!

WINNING THE LEAGUE FOR RANGERS

Saturday 18 April 1959 saw Glasgow in a strange state of puzzlement. Rangers lost 2–1 to Aberdeen at Ibrox, and Celtic beat Hearts 2–1 at Parkhead. Such a combination of results would normally bring great joy for Celtic and dark despair for Rangers, but the problem here was that Celtic's victory gave Rangers the league championship! Both games followed remarkably parallel paths – Rangers and Hearts were both one up at half time (Rangers would have won the championship if these results had stayed unaltered) but then both Aberdeen and Celtic scored twice each, Celtic's goals coming from a deft flick by Bertie Auld and then a diving header from Eric Smith. This meant that although Rangers lost to Aberdeen and were duly booed off the park (deservedly so, according to the press) they had won the league thanks to Celtic. Rangers and Celtic fans alike did not know whether to laugh or to cry!

TEN MEN WON THE LEAGUE

Celtic have won the Scottish League on many occasions often with a degree of excitement, but never surely in more dramatic circumstances than those of Monday 21 May 1979 at a packed Parkhead. This game had originally been scheduled for the New Year but had fallen victim like so many games that bad winter to the weather. It was Celtic's last game of the season, and they had to win it, otherwise the title would be likely to go to Ibrox. Rangers were 1–0 up at half time and then early in the second half Johnny Doyle was sent off by referee Eddie Pringle for foolishly aiming a kick at a Rangers player lying on the ground. Oh dear! A victory seemed so unlikely but Celtic's ten roared into action galvanised by Roy Aitken. Aitken himself scored in a goalmouth scramble, then George McCluskey put Celtic 2–1 up – only for Rangers to equalise. But this Celtic team did not know how to lose, and within the last ten minutes persuaded Rangers' Colin Jackson to score an own goal. With time running out, Murdo MacLeod decided to try for goal from an impossible angle and distance, reckoning that the ball would at least go into the Celtic End and use up valuable seconds – but he scored and Parkhead erupted as it had never done so before!

CELTIC IN WARTIME

In the two terrible wars that were fought in the first half of the twentieth century, the fortunes of Celtic could hardly have shown more of a contrast. In the First World War, they won almost everything; between 1939 and 1945 they won virtually nothing. It is of course very easy to scoff at wartime football, and indeed a great deal of the sport played in Second World War is deemed 'unofficial', but that surely ignores the massive part that football played in the morale of the population not only at home but for those serving overseas. Patsy Gallacher, for example, was described as the 'man most talked about in the trenches' by Scottish troops.

In the 1914–18 conflict, although internationals and the Scottish Cup were suspended, the Scottish League continued as did the two Glasgow competitions. Willie Maley was able, to a large extent, to make sure that all his fine team of 1914 had vital jobs in the munitions industries on the

Clyde and therefore were not likely to be called up until later in the war. As a result, the league championship was won in 1915, 1916, 1917 and 1919 (Rangers won it narrowly in 1918), the Glasgow Cup in 1915/16 and 1916/17, and the Glasgow Charity Cup for seven years in a row from 1912 until 1918. 1915/16 and 1916/17 therefore join 1907/08 and 1966/67 as the years in which Celtic won every competition they entered.

Several remarkable things happened during the First World War. A defeat by Hearts at Tynecastle on 13 November 1915 was distressing, but if the supporters had known that their next defeat would not be until the Scottish League game at Celtic Park to Kilmarnock on 21 April 1917, they would have been less downhearted. The unbeaten run lasted 75 games – 66 League, 3 Glasgow Cup and 2 Glasgow Charity Cup games, although they did lose in May 1916 to the Rest of the League in a friendly played for the Belgian Refugee Fund at Hampden.

On 15 April 1916 they were compelled because of war restrictions to play two games in one day. This was by no means unique but Celtic are the only team to have done this and won the pair of them, clinching the league championship in the process! At 3.30 p.m. they kicked off at Celtic Park against Raith Rovers, beat them convincingly 6–0 (thereby creating a new record for scoring goals in a season) then, without changing out of their strips, travelled by charabanc (several hundreds of their supporters took the train) to Motherwell to defeat them 3–1 in a game that kicked off at 6.15 p.m. and finished in moonlight! The only change of personnel was Joe Cassidy as centre forward for Joe O'Kane. That Celtic team was so good that it was reckoned that even if Raith Rovers and Motherwell had put up 22 men against them at the same time, Celtic would still have won! The

Glasgow Herald was awestruck in admiration for all this, not least because, 'if football had been the dishonest business that it is sometimes portrayed to be' Celtic could have lost the game at Motherwell, thereby prolonging interest in the league championship and earning more money. But Maley's side were simply not made that way!

In the Second World War, on the other hand, there was very little to cheer the Celtic faithful. The ageing and ailing Maley was at last prevailed upon to retire in early 1940 when he has not far short of his 72nd birthday and had exhausted himself on building his beloved Celtic virtually all his life. The problem was that he had not trained a successor, and Jimmy McStay, the excellent captain of a decade earlier, was appointed manager without really appreciating what the job entailed. In addition, there were the difficult times of war, and Rangers had done what Celtic did in the First World War, namely ensured that most of their best players were in war-related work and therefore available to play.

Celtic, even without their star man Jimmy Delaney (injured with a broken arm) for the first two years of the war, really should have done better. The Southern Division of the Scottish League was never won, nor was the Southern League Cup nor the Summer Cup, and the only two successes came in the Glasgow Cup of September 1940 when they beat Rangers 1–0 in the final thanks to a Joe Gillan goal, and the Glasgow Charity Cup of May 1943 when they beat Third Lanark 3–0. Apart from that there was little for Celtic fans to be happy about.

There was also the awful occasion of New Year's Day 1943. Granted, far more important events were happening in North Africa and Stalingrad, but Celtic fans all over the world were distressed to hear the news that Celtic had lost 8–1 to Rangers at Ibrox. This result, of course, beats Celtic's 7–1 victory in 1957 so it is just as well perhaps that wartime football is considered unofficial!

EIGHT GAMES IN TWELVE DAYS WINS THE LEAGUE

The dreadful events of the Hampden Riot of 1909 meant that the Scottish Cup was withheld. It is a shame that that terrible event tends to mean that fewer Celtic fans know about how the team won the Scottish League that season. Beginning on the night of Monday 19 April, the very night that the SFA met to decide that there would be no replay of the Scottish Cup final, Celtic played eight games in twelve days to win the league, beating Hearts, Morton, Motherwell, Queen's Park and Hamilton, drawing with Hamilton and Airdrie and losing only to Hibs. They played on Monday, Wednesday, Thursday, Saturday, Monday, Wednesday, Thursday and Friday to earn enough points to win the Championship and pip Dundee who could only stand and watch in admiration and awe. With Sunny Jim, Jimmy McMenemy and Jimmy Quinn on board, no task was too much for Maley's men!

The reason for playing so many fixtures in such a short time was that the season in those days finished rigidly at the end of April for reasons bound up with players' wages and close-season tours. Celtic had had a few games postponed for reasons of bad weather and international fixtures and there had been a remarkable amount of replays in the Glasgow Cup in the autumn, and the Scottish Cup final itself had of course used up two Saturdays.

Celtic were clearly not too exhausted after their efforts, for the day after they won the league by beating Hamilton at Douglas Park (the evening of 30 April), they played a charity match in Aberdeen and then travelled to Fort William on Monday 3 May to play the North of Scotland in another charity match.

WILLIE O'NEILL

Willie O'Neill, who died in 2011, was mainly a reserve, but a fine one. He is chiefly remembered for two things – one was his sudden elevation to play in the Scottish Cup final of 1961 after Jim Kennedy was stricken with appendicitis, a painful experience for Celtic, although O'Neill did not disgrace himself – and the other was the Scottish League Cup final of October 1966. Fifteen minutes remained and Celtic were desperately hanging on to a 1–0 lead given to them through a Lennox goal in the first half. Rangers' Alex Smith was put through but he did not get a clean hit on the ball. It was, however, good enough to beat Ronnie Simpson and the ball was tricking agonisingly towards the goal line. It was one of those times when time stands still and your whole life passes in front of you, particularly for the 50,000 of us standing behind that goal. Slowly, slowly it trickled goalwards. It was going to be one of the softest goals of all time, but then out of nowhere appeared Willie O'Neill to turn it round the post for a corner. Ronnie Simpson patted him on the head, Billy McNeill said 'Well done' and we all breathed a collective sigh of relief. The corner was dealt with, and Celtic held out for a 1–0 victory. It was Willie's moment of glory and the poetic among us said 'Cometh the hour, cometh the man!' or as Scottish grannies would say, 'Ilka doggie has his day.'

THE BITTER SWEET
YEAR OF 1970

Rarely has there been such a roller-coaster of emotions as Celtic supporters experienced in 1970. The Scottish League was won as early as 28 March in a goalless draw at Tynecastle, and Rangers had been defeated in the Scottish Cup quarter-final more than a month earlier. Progress was being made in the European Cup with Fiorentina defeated and Leeds United awaited.

But then came the Scottish Cup final, and a defeat to Aberdeen in which three key refereeing decisions by the infamous Bobby Davidson turned the game – a penalty awarded to Aberdeen when the ball hit Bobby Murdoch's chest, a goal disallowed for Celtic and a penalty not awarded to Celtic when most commentators were convinced there should have been. Even so, as Stein himself always said, you really have to be so far ahead that refereeing decisions don't matter.

A few days after that, euphoria returned with the glorious defeat of Leeds United at Hampden Park before a record crowd for the European Cup to put Celtic into the final for the second time in four years. But oh! That final! Complacency – 'the serpent of complacency' as distinguished historians put it – crept into paradise, Feyenoord were taken far too lightly, the team played well below themselves and paid the penalty for their folly. Maybe the wrong team formation was used, maybe John Hughes should have scored that goal, maybe the team were upset by the perpetual noise from the horns of the Dutch, maybe if they had held out for a replay it would have been a different story, but no-one could have said that Celtic were the better team, even though they scored first. Then with crass tactlessness, the players announced that they were forming a consortium – to make more money!

Clearly heads had swollen! And what happened on that awful tour of America? No-one wanted to be there for the team were now only second best in Europe! Stein suddenly disappeared back to Glasgow, Gemmell and Auld were sent home, the performances of the team were half-hearted and mediocre, and everyone was glad to get it over with.

The fans were mystified and rumours flew around Glasgow about the real reason for the loss of the European Cup and serious speculation went on about the future of Jock Stein and so many of his team, who were, after all, still the best in Britain as the defeat of Leeds United proved. And the fans stayed loyal. The football season started again in August, the team with new faces beginning to be introduced did well, but the year of 1970 finished on a bad note with the loss of the Scottish League Cup final to Rangers (who thus won their first honour since 1966) in October, and Aberdeen were comfortable at the top of the league, having beaten Celtic at Parkhead in December. Yes, it was a difficult year.

FEAR OF FLYING

Jimmy Johnstone was afraid of flying. So indeed, are a lot people. It is something, however, that can be coped with. One takes a deep breath, grits one's teeth, thinks positive thoughts and gets through it. The trouble with Jimmy was that he was the greatest player in the world on his day, and therefore neurotic whingings tended to be taken more seriously even by the formidable Jock Stein. On one famous occasion in

November 1968, the situation was manipulated by both Jock and Jimmy to everyone's advantage.

Celtic were playing Red Star Belgrade in the European Cup, the first leg being at Parkhead on 13 November. Jimmy was not keen on going to Belgrade a fortnight later, so Jock said that if Celtic were three goals or more to the good, he might not have to go. 67,000 were at Parkhead that night to see one of Johnstone's best performances. He teamed-up brilliantly with his friend Bobby Murdoch and scored two goals (one of them a magnificent solo effort) as Celtic won 5–1. He also had a hand in all the other three and ran off the field shouting, 'I'll no need tae go!' Indeed, he stayed at home for the second leg which Celtic drew comfortably.

On other occasions, Jimmy's pleas to Jock were less successful with, 'You'll get on that f***in' plane like everybody else!' being the normal riposte. But Jock would detail the ever-willing banter merchant Willie O'Neill to sit beside Jimmy and tell him dirty jokes to keep his mind off things. Jimmy would himself joke, 'I'm no feart o' flying . . . just crashing!' There is little doubt, however, that one of the reasons why Jimmy was ludicrously undercapped by Scotland was that he often found some excuse or other to dodge away fixtures.

PETER SCARFF

Tuberculosis has, thankfully, been more or less eradicated from the developed world at least. In the 1930s TB, or consumption as it was called, was a dreadful scourge, and this came home to Celtic when Peter Scarff, one of the heroes of the 1931 Scottish Cup final (the forward line read R. Thomson,

A. Thomson, McGrory, Scarff and Napier) coughed up blood one day after training in early 1932. Peter died at the Bridge of Weir Sanatorium in December 1933.

OVER THE LINE

Celtic have been involved in more than their fair share of controversial incidents over the years, none more so than a game at Tannadice Park, Dundee, on 1 September 1962. Celtic needed a win to qualify from their section of the Scottish League Cup and halfway through the second half, had the ball quite clearly over the line in a goalmouth scramble before left-half Stewart Fraser kicked the ball out again. Neither the referee, nor the linesman gave the goal, but it was obvious that the ball was over, an opinion shared by a photographer, a policeman and apparently by Fraser himself in later years. It happened at the Shed End of Tannadice in front of the Celtic fans whose mood was not improved when the game finished 0–0 and Celtic lost out on qualification to Hearts who beat Dundee at Tynecastle that day.

THE FASTEST HAT-TRICK

On 14 March 1936 in a 5–0 win over Motherwell, Jimmy McGrory scored a hat-trick in three minutes, earning the nickname 'goal-a-minute'. This hat-trick came between the 65th and 67th minute and is arguably the fastest hat-trick of all time. One goal came from the work of Jimmy Delaney and the other two from the wing play of Frank Murphy.

This came in McGrory's great season in which he beat the goalscoring records of Steve Bloomer and Hughie Ferguson and scored 50 League goals.

> And wait a bit, don't be so fast
> We've left the star turn to the last
> There in the midst of all his glory
> Goal-a-minute James McGrory!

ARTHURLIE

In the same way that Inverness Caledonian Thistle haunted Celtic in the early years of the twenty-first century, the name Arthurlie sent shivers of horror down the spines of all Celtic fans who were alive in 1897. This was because of a horrendous 4–2 defeat in the Scottish Cup at Dunterlie Park on 9 January 1897. The pitch was bad but that was only part of the story, for the main reason was internal dissension in the team. Celtic's two great stars of the age – Sandy McMahon and Dan Doyle – were both missing; Sandy was injured and Dan simply didn't turn up for reasons that were never explained. But good came out of bad, because a few months later Willie Maley was appointed as secretary/manager.

MERRY CHRISTMAS

Until recent times Christmas Day was just an ordinary working day in Scotland and if it fell on a Saturday, football was played as normal. On at least four occasions, Celtic had a particularly Merry Christmas. In 1909 they won 1–0 at Kilmarnock thanks to a wonderful Jimmy Quinn goal as he charged the length of the field beating man after man in the mud. In 1937 Kilmarnock came to Celtic Park under their new manager Jimmy McGrory and were put to the sword 8–0. In 1965 Celtic played scintillating football to beat Morton 8–1 to entertain 21,000 fans at Celtic Park. In 1971, also at home, in a fine game of football Celtic beat Hearts 3–2.

ALL THE TROPHIES
IN A MONTH

April 1969 was a remarkable month. A fire at Hampden in October 1968 meant that the Scottish League Cup final was postponed until 5 April 1969. A glorious display of attacking football saw Celtic beat Hibs 6–2 and win the League Cup; on 21 April a draw at Kilmarnock was enough to clinch the league championship and then on 26 April in the Scottish Cup final, Celtic beat Rangers 4–0 in one of their best ever cup final displays, and thus all the domestic trophies had been secured within three weeks!

ALBERT KIDD

Albert is one of the heroes of Celtic, yet he never played for them! His career had struggled and he was probably heading for obscurity when destiny called upon him on that fateful day of 3 May 1986. Hearts and Dundee were drawing 1–1 at Dens Park, something that would have given the Jambos the championship in spite of Celtic's hammering of St Mirren. And then Albert came on and scored two goals (one of them a real cracker) to give Dundee a 2–0 victory and Celtic the championship. At Ibrox, the Rangers fans cheered when they heard that Kidd had scored, thinking that it was Walter Kidd of Hearts rather than the lesser-known Albert of Dundee whom it would be fair to say that very few people had heard until his moment of immortality.

CELTIC'S COLDEST EVER GAME?

Winter in Scotland can of course be cold, but December 2010 was reckoned to be, by any standards, bad. On midwinter's night of 21 December with the temperature given as -8°C, 44,522 watched Celtic take on Kilmarnock, Thomas Rogne heading a late equaliser to earn Celtic a 1–1 draw. This game cannot be proved beyond doubt to be Celtic's coldest ever game, but those who were there would have supreme confidence in putting it forward for the honour. Scottish football is not of course for 'softies'!

SUNNY JIM THE GOALIE

Sunny Jim Young was a mighty man who dominated and inspired Celtic in the great days of the Edwardian era. Normally a right-half but very versatile, he was a great man to have around. In the early days of 1909, his versatility took on another dimension. Sunny was injured and was upset to miss the game against Rangers at Ibrox on Friday 1 January 1909, a game which Celtic nevertheless won 3–1. But in that game, goalkeeper Davie Adams was injured, and Celtic did not have a goalkeeper handy for their game at Kilmarnock the following day, and on New Year's night it would have been no easy matter to find another in time. Sunny then approached Maley with a suggestion. His ankle was improving and although he could not play in his normal midfield role, why couldn't he play in goal? Maley reluctantly agreed, for there was no other option, and Sunny played in goal. Sadly, the team lost 3–1 but the *Glasgow Herald* says that Young coped 'admirably'.

TONY CASCARINO

Just what was this fellow's problem? He's still seen on Sky TV talking knowledgeably about the game, but could he play himself? Supporters of Millwall, Aston Villa, Chelsea, Olympique de Marseilles and the Republic of Ireland may well think he could, but Celtic supporters who were around in the 1991/92 season may beg to difer. He had a remarkable game on 5 October 1991. Relegated to the bench for his inability to score goals, he was brought on as a substitute for Charlie Nicholas in a game against Hearts at Parkhead, scored his first ever goal for the club with a miskick and then got sent off for throwing a punch at Craig Levein! All in the space of 15 minutes! You couldn't really make that up, could you?

1963/64 THE YEAR OF THE RANGERS COMPLEX

The season of 1963/64 was in fact a good season for Celtic with many fine performances and a good run in Europe which took them to the semi-final of the European Cup Winners' Cup. The problem was Rangers to whom Celtic lost five times: 3–0 twice in the League Cup in August, 2–1 in the league in September, 1–0 in the league on New Year's Day and 2–0 in the Scottish Cup in March. An analysis of each of the five games reveals an astonishingly similar pattern of Celtic being well on top in the first half-hour, but failing to make their advantage count, then a cruel break in the shape of a refereeing decision, a defensive error or an apparently net-bound shot hitting the post. A collapse would then follow and the collective belief that spread throughout the dressing room, the board room and the terracing that, somehow or other, Celtic were not allowed by some malevolent deity to beat Rangers. Rangers won the treble in 1964 but made absolutely no impact on Europe which leads historians to wonder how they would have done in Scotland if Celtic had showed more belief in themselves. It took Jock Stein to rid Celtic of this death wish.

THE YEAR AFTER THE YEAR BEFORE

Everyone knows how good 1967 was. Some of us think that the spring of 1968 (and 1969 for that matter as well), although showing less obvious success in terms of trophies, revealed a great deal more about the character of that great side. In 1967/68 although the League Cup had been won, there had been major disappointments as the team blew up in the first round of the European Cup against Dinamo Kiev and in the first round of the Scottish Cup against Dunfermline, leading to all sorts of suggestions of 'one-season wonders', 'flukes', etc. There was also of course the South American fiasco which reflected no credit on anyone.

The Scottish League also seemed to have gone when goalkeeping errors gave Rangers an undeserved draw at Parkhead on 2 January 1968. Rangers were two points ahead and as the teams played each other only twice, Celtic would have no other opportunity to beat them. They were indeed 'needing snookers' in the shape of other teams beating Rangers, and this did not look like happening.

But psychology now played a part. Stein realised that if Celtic kept winning and winning well by playing brilliant football, Rangers under a new, inexperienced and raw manager called Davie White, would crack under the pressure. Charlie Gallagher and Jim Brogan were brought into the team, great victories, particularly away from home in a four-in-a-row run at St Johnstone, Dundee United, Hearts and Aberdeen were recorded and you could almost hear the Rangers edifice buckling. Their withdrawal from the Glasgow Cup (apart from being an insult to a grand old tournament) allowed Celtic supporters to claim that Rangers were afraid of Celtic, and then Dundee United, smarting from their 5–0 defeat by Celtic a few days previously and looking to redeem themselves in the eyes of their supporters, took a point off Rangers to bring their lead down to one point.

Then Morton on the night of 17 April, while Celtic were winning the Glasgow Cup (which Rangers had scorned) in a wonderful 8–0 defeat of Clyde, did the same and thus the teams were level on points but Celtic had a far superior goal average. The same Morton then almost took a point off Celtic, but Bobby Lennox scored a scrappy goal in the last minute to keep Celtic ahead, and then Rangers, their confidence shattered, folded in their final league game of the season to Aberdeen at Ibrox.

Celtic thus won the league while watching the Scottish Cup final (Dunfermline beat Hearts 3–1) and that must be some sort of record as well! The final word on this remarkable season must come concerning John Fallon, the Celtic-daft redhead who had the misfortune to concede the two goals to Rangers which for so long looked as if they had lost us the league. On the pivotal night of 17 April, he was playing at Parkhead in a reserve match against Raith Rovers. Ball boys kept telling him the score at Morton and Hampden, and he left the field at Parkhead that night neither knowing nor caring what the score was in the game in which he had been playing!

PENALTY SHOOT-OUTS

It would be a fair statement that Celtic and penalty shoot-outs do not go well together. Three particular horror stories spring to mind. One was the European Cup semi-final at Parkhead on 19 April 1972 when after 90 goalless minutes at the San Siro, another 90 goalless minutes at Parkhead and then another 30 minutes of extra time at Parkhead, a penalty shoot-out was ordered. There were nine saints and one sinner, the unfortunate man being Dixie Deans who took Celtic's first penalty and put it over the bar. A few heartless morons barracked and booed him, but Dixie only took seventeen days to go from zero to hero when on 6 May he scored his famous hat-trick for Celtic in the 1972 Scottish Cup final against Hibs.

A less happy Scottish Cup final came on 12 May 1990 which saw a poor Celtic side play above themselves to earn a deserved 0–0 draw with favourites Aberdeen. Extra time failed to separate the sides and the cup went to penalties for the first time ever. Both teams were better at taking penalties than in the other skills of the game that day, and the final score ending up 9–8 for Aberdeen with Dariusz Wdowczyk and Anton Rogan being the unlucky Celtic players who missed. It was a painful cup final, but had we known what would happen to Aberdeen over the next 20 years, we might not have been quite so jealous of them. Indeed most decent Aberdeen supporters admitted that it was a dreadful way to win the Scottish Cup.

And then we come to that awful day of 27 November 1994 and the Scottish League Cup final between Celtic and First Division Raith Rovers. It was vital to Celtic in that, although the wicked old board had been ousted and a new regime was in place, success was not yet coming to Tommy Burns and the League Cup was badly needed to kick-start the season. It was a good game, played at Ibrox because Celtic were playing their home games at Hampden that season. Raith went ahead, then Andy Walker equalised with a fine header before Charlie Nicholas scored what looked like the deserved winner late in the game. Sadly, Gordon Marshall could not hold a Jason Dair drive and Gordon Dalziel headed home an equaliser. Extra time, fruitless and futile with two tired teams followed, and we moved to the penalty shoot-out. It was 5–5 before sudden death became necessary and after Raith scored to make it 6–5, Paul McStay, by some distance the best Scottish player of that era, had the misfortune to have his effort saved by goalkeeper Scott Thomson. No-one could really begrudge the Kirkcaldy men their one and only moment of glory, but for Celtic the pain was intense and long-lasting.

CELTIC'S HOME CUP FINAL

Celtic Park has hosted the Scottish Cup final on a number of occasions – 1913, 1921, 1993 and 1998 for example – when for one reason or another Hampden Park or Ibrox was not available. But in 1902, Celtic Park had to be used even though Celtic were one of the competing teams. 5 April 1902 saw the terrible Ibrox disaster in which 26 people lost their lives at the international between Scotland and England, and it was hardly appropriate to use Ibrox for the Scottish Cup final between Celtic and Hibs so soon after the tragedy. The new Hampden was still being built (it would open in 1903) and the old Hampden was deemed too small now for a Scottish Cup final crowd. Thus it was that Celtic Park was deployed for Celtic v Hibs. It was a far from happy occasion for Celtic lost 1–0 to the team that some regarded as the 'parent club', but it is to be hoped that Hibs enjoyed winning the Scottish Cup of 1902, for 110 years further on Hibs have failed to win it again. However, the joke that the last time Hibs won the Scottish Cup, Edinburgh was granted a half-holiday by the delighted Mary Queen of Scots, is not quite true. But in 1902 their players certainly ruffled a few Celtic feathers by adapting the Boer War song 'Goodbye Dolly Gray' to:

Goodbye Celtic, we must leave you
Though it breaks our heart to go
We are off to Embra
The Scottish Cup to show!

GEORGE CONNELLY ENTERTAINS

George Connelly was one of the best natural football players
that Celtic have ever had, and his sad inability to cope with
the emotional side of playing professional football for a top
team in the 1970s was a sad loss to Celtic, Scotland and
himself. But his first public appearance came on 12 January
1966 at half time in a European Cup Winners' Cup game
between Celtic and Dinamo Kiev when he entertained the
fans with a brilliant and prolonged display of ball control. It
was one of Jock Stein's stunts which reflected well on Celtic
and encouraged the (correct) view that Celtic's youngsters
were simply hotching with talent. Before his sad departure
and lapse into depression and alcoholism (honestly detailed
in his book *Celtic's Lost Legend*), George won four Scottish
League medals and three Scottish Cup medals.

McNEILL'S DEPUTIES

One of the sad side-effects of the long-lasting and consistently
brilliant career of Billy McNeill was the exclusion of two
other capable Celtic centre-halves apart from the times
that McNeill was injured. One was John McNamee who
understudied McNeill in the early 1960s and occasionally

played at right-half alongside him before going on to carve out a career for himself with Hibs and Newcastle United. John Cushley was marginally more fortunate. When Billy was out with injuries in 1964/65 and again in 1965/66, John was given a lengthy run in the team and played well without letting anyone down and in 1965/66 played in enough games to earn for himself a Scottish League medal. He went on to play for West Ham United and Dunfermline Athletic, and his other claim to fame, of course, is the trip to Spain as Jimmy McGrory's interpreter in the ill-thought out attempt in August 1964 to sign Alfredo di Stéfano.

QUEEN'S PARK

Often patronisingly looked upon as a quaint relic from a bygone age, the proud amateurs are still with us, albeit now permanently marooned in the lower reaches of the Scottish League. Yet on four occasions in the past fifty years they have given Celtic more than a little embarrassment in the Scottish Cup by playing better and really deserving to win. On 20 February 1965 they played out of their skins at Hampden and for a long time looked like winning the tie until Bobby Lennox scored the only goal of the game. Then, on 11 March 1967 at Parkhead with Celtic still on a high after their defeat of Vojvodina on the Wednesday night previously, Queen's persuaded Tommy Gemmell to score an own goal before 30 seconds had elapsed, then fought tooth and nail and kept the score at 4–3 to Celtic for most of the second half before Bobby Lennox settled the issue. On 15 February 1986 at Parkhead, Queen's scored first again, this time with a penalty kick before the dysfunctional Celtic team settled the nerves of their followers in the meagre 11,656 crowd with goals from Brian McClair and Roy Aitken. Then on 7 February 2009 Celtic were two goals up to Queen's Park thanks to Gary Caldwell and Scott McDonald just before half time, but then 22,223 watched in horror as they proceeded to play rubbish, allowed Queen's Park back into the game with a well taken goal and then struggled through to the final whistle with Queen's pressing constantly and frankly worthy of a draw.

THE GENERAL STRIKE

This event took place in early May 1926, during which time the Glasgow Charity Cup was played. As newspapers were badly affected by the strike, this presents a few problems for the Celtic historian, particularly for the game played against Third Lanark on the middle Saturday of the strike. This was the semi-final between Celtic and Third Lanark at Parkhead. We know that Celtic won 2–0, and an unconfirmed report states that there was a small crowd of 4,000 (who would all, of course, have had to walk to the ground, as indeed would the players). Tommy McInally scored and Willie McStay converted a penalty. A fellow called Gilfillan played, it is said, on the right wing, but we know little else about him.

By the time that the final was played on 15 May at Ibrox, the General Strike was over, and a crowd of 30,000 went to Ibrox to see Celtic beat Queen's Park 2–1 with goals from Tommy McInally and Jimmy McGrory. Queen's Park were, of course, seen as the team of the bosses, the mine owners and the strikebreakers and were booed throughout the game by Celtic fans who sang 'The Red Flag' as well as their various Irish anthems.

THE GHOSTLY PASSENGER

It was 15 May 1963, the night of Celtic's infamous collapse to Rangers in the Scottish Cup final. The 'Midnight Mail' was chugging out of Buchanan Street station to Aberdeen and a group of young fans were sitting disconsolately in their compartment. Staring at the lights of Glasgow gradually being replaced by country, they hadn't noticed a man come in. He started to talk about this being only a temporary set back, and how very soon, the name of Celtic would resound round the world and how nothing would stop them. The boys smiled and laughed trying to get to sleep to allow them to forget the unimaginable horrors they were going though and the ridicule that awaited them at school the following morning. You often got, after all, such drunken men on late night trains. Except this one wasn't drunk. He was exceptionally lucid as he told the boys about how good Celtic were going to be. He kept mentioning Inter Milan, Lisbon and Stein, the current manager of Dunfermline. And then, at some station or other, Larbert perhaps or Stirling, he suddenly disappeared.

WELL, WELL, WELL, IT WAS NEARLY WELL, WELL, WELL

Celtic have had many famous cup final wins, but one of their most famous was a 2–2 draw against Motherwell in 1931. The 'Well were winning 2–0 and we were inside the last ten minutes. Motherwell's fans and their fellow travellers in blue were triumphant while Celtic fans were beginning to head towards the exits. But then a Charlie Napier free-kick found Jimmy McGrory who made it 2–1 and gave Celtic a chance. The game seemed to have run its course when Bertie Thomson sent over a ball looking for the head of McGrory. McGrory went for it, but it was the head of Motherwell defender Alan Craig which diverted the ball into his own net. As Celtic celebrated, Craig lay on the ground thumping the turf, inconsolable and desolate, before the ever-gentlemanly Jimmy McGrory helped him to his feet and said that he would see him in the replay on Wednesday. Celtic won the replay 4–2, but from the way that the Celtic fans celebrated on the night of the 2–2 draw, one would have thought that they had won the cup already.

INDUSTRIAL ACTION

Threats of strikes and industrial action do not go well with professional football. It is of course not uncommon for an individual player to take the huff, fall out with his manager, act like a spoiled brat and walk out, but for a whole team to threaten industrial action is a very rare happening indeed. It has, however, happened at least three times in Celtic's history with dire consequences. One was on 2 May 1942 before the Southern League Cup semi-final against Rangers at Hampden when the players were told on the team bus at St Enoch's Square that there were to be no complimentary tickets for friends and relatives who would have therefore to pay at the turnstiles. The players were all for refusing to strip, but the directors held firm and the players caved in both in the dressing room and on the field where they lost 2–0 to Rangers in an astonishingly weak performance.

Another came in August 1998 when a dispute about bonus money was allowed to become public and heels were dug in. Fergus McCann, who did not become a millionaire by being dictated to, told his players to have a 'reality check' and gave a large donation to Yorkhill Hospital, thus emotionally blackmailing the players into doing the same. During this dispute Celtic went out of the European Champions League and the Scottish League Cup in weak displays to Croatia Zagreb and Airdrie, so that no bonus money would have been paid anyway!

The circumstances were totally different in 1896, for the cause in dispute was the 'freedom of the press', a concept dear to Victorian hearts. On 21 November Celtic had lost the Glasgow Cup to Rangers, and had been criticised for foul play in the press, the *Scottish Referee* and the *Evening Times* in particular who had said things like 'fouls were numerous' and 'Celtic were always the aggressors'. The players resented this and when they turned up for the next game against Hibs at Parkhead on 28 November they refused to play unless the offending journalists were removed from the press box. Celtic's committee refused to do this, and a total strike seemed likely. Eventually eight of the players agreed to play but Peter Meehan, John Divers and Barney Battles still held out, Battles in particular hurting from the sarcastic 'gentle Barney' moniker applied to him. Celtic managed to field eleven men – one reserve was on hand, another was summoned from Hampden in a horse and carriage in time for the second half, and committee man Willie Maley (who thought he had retired) was prevailed upon to play. In the circumstances, the team did well to hold Hibs to a 1–1 draw, but the three miscreants seldom played again (with the exception of Battles who eventually made his peace with the club after brief spells at Dundee and

Liverpool) and player discontent continued. The dreadful defeat at Arthurlie in January 1897 was not unconnected with this affair, one feels, but the net result was a good one of the appointment in April 1897 of Willie Maley as secretary/manager on a salary.

In this context, we must also mention the ludicrous events of 27 November 2010 when the Scottish referees went on strike for all sorts of reasons of 'lack of respect' and 'unwarranted criticism', etc. Everyone knew that Celtic were being got at here, the events not unconnected with a game at Tannadice a month earlier when a referee changed his mind about awarding a penalty, but the SPL laudably refused to be blackmailed and brought in foreign referees. Celtic thus played Inverness Caledonian Thistle under the tutelage of a Luxembourg referee called Alain Hamer who came on to the field to a warm round of applause (extremely rare at Parkhead for a referee) and who had a good game. Celtic didn't though, for defensive errors cost them two points.

FRANK CONNOR

This man kept coming and going to Celtic Park like a yoyo, and would appear to have a strong claim to being the greatest manager Celtic ever had in that he never lost a match, beating Dundee and Sporting Lisbon (managed by Bobby Robson) and drawing with Hibs in the interregnum between Liam Brady and Lou Macari from 8 October to 26 October 1993. This was all the more commendable when one considers that the club was then under the crass stewardship of the old regime of directors only months away from their spectacular Waterloo. Macari's first game saw Celtic win at Ibrox, and that team was picked by Frank Connor, a man by whom all the players swore.

Swore? Ah yes, it was rumoured that the odd 'bad word' sometimes escaped the lips of the bluff, brusque but totally likeable Frank, so much so that when he was manager at Raith Rovers, supporters standing in the queue for their pies and Bovril at the back of the main stand could hear the half-time tirade being delivered at full volume and not without the odd earthy choice of expression if the Rovers were not doing so well!

A goalkeeper by trade, he joined the club in 1960, was freed in May 1961 but brought back in July 1961 before being given his annual free transfer again in May 1962. He was brought in by Jock Stein as a coach in autumn 1977, lasted three years before moving to Berwick Rangers, but then was brought back to be assistant manager to Davie Hay in summer 1983. Hay surprisingly sacked him in February 1986, but then Liam Brady brought him back in summer 1993. In between all of this, he played, coached and managed a myriad of teams.

Many supporters (and most of the players) thought that he would have been a better manager than Lou Macari in that awful winter of 1993/94.

SPATS AND FISTICUFFS

It is of course by no means uncommon in football teams for passions to get a little heated at training sessions and even for blows to be struck. Supporters heard various stories about Jimmy Quinn in the old days, and there was the famous one in 1957 when Bobby Evans and Charlie Tully had a difference of opinion about a newspaper article written by Tully which seemed to criticise Evans. This dispute was settled so spectacularly by captain Bertie Peacock that Celtic then went out and whipped Rangers 7–1 in the Scottish League Cup final a few days later!

Stories were leaked in the late 1990s about Tosh McKinlay and Henrik Larsson not seeing eye-to-eye, but rather head-to-head. So much so, that Tosh was lauded by the fans at Ibrox:

> Oh Tosh McKinlay
> Tosh, Tosh, Tosh, Tosh McKinlay
> He put the heid
> Upon the Swede
> Oh, Tosh McKinlay!

In December 2006 at the full-time whistle at Dunfermline Neil Lennon and Aiden McGeady were seen having a 'handbags moment' pushing each other around, after Celtic had beaten the Pars 2–1. What would have happened if they had lost? The same Aiden McGeady also fell out with Artur Boruc at Lennoxtown in 2009. No great harm came of these silly incidents, hard though the media tried, but on the other hand considerable damage was done to the club by what happened in the dressing room at half time at Ibrox on New Year's Day 1963, at McDiarmid Park on 6 October 1993 and at Parkhead on the awful night of the Inverness catastrophe on 8 February 2000. All these occasions (we are told) involved members of the management team as well as players.

CHARLIE NICHOLAS

Few players have caused such distress as Charlie Nicholas. Never afraid to call himself 'Celtic-minded' and on one famous occasion caught off camera by Sky TV cheering a Celtic goal, Charlie nevertheless caused a tremendous amount of distress in 1983 when he allowed himself to be persuaded by the press, a grasping agent and a venal Celtic board to leave Celtic Park for Arsenal, ignoring the plaintive appeals of the fans, including one which said simply 'Don't go, Charlie'. His three-year career for Celtic (even though one of them was badly disrupted by a broken leg) had old-timers comparing him with Patsy Gallacher, and who knows what he could have done if he had stayed? As it is, he went to Arsenal and Aberdeen before eventually coming back in 1990. But this was no Tommy McInally type of return. He had the misfortune to be there in the dark early 1990s, and did little to relieve the gloom. Now much ridiculed for his ungrammatical and occasionally patronising style of punditry on Sky TV, nevertheless the main emotion engendered by Charlie is one of sadness for a lost career with even a feeling that another European Cup might have been won if Charlie Nicholas had stayed in harness with Paul McStay and under the guidance of Billy McNeill.

HAMPDEN OUR HOME

Hampden Park is of course sometimes known as the National Stadium, but it ought to have a special place in the hearts of Celtic fans as well. Celtic played in the first game there on

31 October 1903, appeared in the first Scottish Cup final there on 16 April 1904 (the day of Jimmy Quinn's hat-trick) and have had loads of subsequent triumphs there in cup finals and other occasions. Hampden has been Celtic's home on the odd time that Parkhead has been redeveloped, notably 1994/95 – by no means one of Celtic's best, although it did end with a Scottish Cup triumph over Airdrie – and several times in Celtic's glory years. Hampden was pressed into service for the World Club Championship against Racing Club of Argentina on 18 October 1967, for the European Cup semi-final against Leeds United on 15 April 1970 (which produced a European Cup record attendance of 135,826) and for the European Cup quarter-final game against Ajax on 24 March 1971. One could argue that the 1971 occasion was because of ground redevelopments at Parkhead, but the other two were for the ill-disguised purpose of a bigger attendance and more money.

CHEATS

One is reluctant to use the word 'cheat' to describe opponents and referees. After all, a referee can make a decision with which one disagrees without being a cheat. Similarly opponents can be guilty of a few robust tackles or charges without being cheats. But there have been two opponents on the European scene who cannot really avoid the word. I refer to Atlético Madrid in 1974 and Rapid Vienna in 1984 – and the sad thing was that both got away with it.

Atlético Madrid came to Celtic Park on 10 April 1974 for the European Cup semi-final with no intention other than to kick Celtic off the park. Managed by the Argentinian Juan

Carlos Lorenzo, Atlético filled their side with thugs and duly got a 0–0 draw even though three were sent off. The loss of three players was not a major problem because they were not their best players and were replaced by others for the second leg. It was rumoured, however, that a Celtic player, with the connivance of the Glasgow police who looked the other way, managed to land 'a dull one' on a Spanish thug in the tunnel at the end of the game. Then for the second leg in Madrid, death threats were issued to Jimmy Johnstone, and as Spain was still a vicious dictatorship with Franco, the erstwhile ally of Hitler and Mussolini, still in power, these were taken seriously. Celtic lost 2–0, but some sort of justice was done when the Spaniards were beaten by Bayern Munich in the final.

But then we had Rapid Vienna in November 1984. In a rough match, Celtic nevertheless won 3–0 and having lost 3–1 in Vienna, qualified for the next round – or so everyone thought. But a brilliant actor called Weinhofer managed to convince the gullible that he had been hit by a bottle, even though TV evidence proved otherwise, and a replay was ordered at least 200 miles from Glasgow, at Old Trafford, Manchester. Hardly surprisingly, an over-emotional Celtic lost, and were cheated out of Europe. Once again, however, the cheats did not totally triumph for they lost to Everton in the final of the UEFA Cup, with the Everton support supplemented by quite a few wearing green and white favours. Although Rapid and Atlético have since been to Glasgow and behaved, their names will forever be tainted by these outrages.

JOE MILLER

It would have to be said that Joe Miller's career at Celtic Park was a disappointment. He arrived from Aberdeen in November 1987 and played his part in the centenary season, but from then on as the team wilted, Joe's form deteriorated badly and he was much criticised and excoriated by the support, not least because he seemed to have only one foot! But he had his moment of glory as well, and this came in the Scottish Cup final of 1989 when a pass-back from Rangers' Gary Stevens held up a little (Rangers would claim improbably afterwards that the grass hadn't been cut properly) and Joe nipped in to score what proved to be the only goal of the game.

THE KILMARNOCK HOODOO

Do hoodoos exist in football? Well, yes and no. Probably (though I am no expert in such matters) the supernatural is not too interested in who wins football matches, but that is not to say that some players and supporters do not believe in such things. Hibs, for example, have not won the Scottish Cup since 1902 and many of their supporters seem to think that some sort of tinker's hex plays a part. But hoodoos should be broken some time, and in this context, historically minded Celtic fans should really worry about a visit of Kilmarnock to Celtic Park. Kilmarnock last won here on 10 December 1955 with two goals from Davie Curlett – and have not repeated that success since! One fears they have to do so soon. They beat Celtic of course in the 2012 Scottish League Cup final, but that was at Hampden. It was the first time they had beaten Celtic in Glasgow since 1957 when they beat them in a Scottish Cup semi-final replay.

VERY WEE JIMMY JOHNSTONE

Everyone knew that Jimmy Johnstone was small, and when he played in the first game of the 1963 Scottish Cup final, he impressed and was universally referred to as 'Wee Jimmy Johnstone'. But the week after that game, Celtic were at Tannadice Park to play Dundee United with the local fans all agog to see 'Wee Jimmy Johnstone'. A gasp arose from the crowd when a wee red-headed boy ran out with the team.

'He's surely not as small as all that!'

No indeed, he wasn't. This was the 3-year-old mascot with red hair and his green and white strip, accompanying Billy McNeill. The 'real' Jimmy Johnstone ran out with the rest of the team. He was still rather small, it has to be said, but still a bit taller than a 3-year-old!

WHY, ALEC, WHY?

Alec Bennett was as good a right winger as Celtic have ever had. Considering that puts him in the same category as Jimmy Delaney and Jimmy Johnstone, that is no mean compliment. Commonly known as 'The Artful Dodger' after the well-known character in Charles Dickens' *Oliver Twist*, Alec played a decisive part in the success of the Celtic team of 1907 and 1908, teaming-up well with his friend Jimmy McMenemy to produce a devastating right-wing combination as Celtic swept the boards of Scottish honours and rightly earned the title of the best in the world.

Why, then, did Alec suddenly jump ship and join Rangers? As another Dickens character Sam Weller in *The Pickwick Papers* would put it, 'There are things that a fella just simply can't understand.'

THE UNCERTAIN FUTURE

Celtic, like the rest of Scottish football, faces in the summer of 2012 an uncertain future. The demise of Rangers, perhaps temporary but possibly permanent, has produced more than a little glee in Celtic-supporting circles. But how are Celtic going to respond to all this? Are they now to apply to join an English League, will they soldier on in Scotland with a support and budget embarrassingly larger than anyone else's, or will Rangers some day come back? One would like to think that another Scottish team, Aberdeen being the most likely one or perhaps Hearts, might seize the opportunity to challenge Celtic on a permanent basis. But will they? One fears that embarrassing exits at an early stage from Europe, more supine transfers of star players and dismal attendances might become even more prevalent. As Scotland's most famous poet put it:

'But och, I backward cast my een on prospects drear
And forrit, though I cannae see, I guess and fear . . .'

Celtic's fans demand that they respond to the new situation. They have a song now which refers to 'the past, the present and the future'. Yes indeed, Celtic are a continuum.

NINE CHAMPIONSHIPS NEVER WON AT PARKHEAD

Celtic won a record-breaking nine league championships in a row between 1966 and 1974, but the funny thing was that none of them were won at Celtic Park. The closest was in 1971 in what was technically a Celtic home game but was played at Hampden because Celtic Park was undergoing renovations to the main stand. On the other occasions, the league was won at other grounds, although in some cases, the league had already been won by opponents slipping up on previous occasions. In 1968, for instance, Dunfermline would have needed to beat Celtic 16–0 to give the championship to Rangers. In 1969, Celtic's draw at Kilmarnock did not mathematically guarantee them the championship, for Rangers might technically have caught them but they went down at Dens Park, Dundee, the following night. The nine occasions were:

7 May 1966	Fir Park	Motherwell 0–1 Celtic
6 May 1967	Ibrox	Rangers 2–2 Celtic
30 April 1968	East End Park	Dunfermline 1–2 Celtic
21 April 1969	Rugby Park	Kilmarnock 2–2 Celtic
28 March 1970	Tynecastle	Hearts 0–0 Celtic
29 April 1971	Hampden	Celtic 2–0 Ayr United
15 April 1972	Bayview	East Fife 0–3 Celtic
28 April 1973	Easter Road	Hibs 0–3 Celtic
27 April 1974	Brockville	Falkirk 1–1 Celtic